New Classics

Kraft Kitchens

New Classics
Our most requested recipes made simple

Random House Canada

National Library of Canada Cataloguing in Publication
New classics : our most requested recipes made simple / Kraft Kitchens.
Includes index.
ISBN 0-679-31219-6

1. Cookery. I. Kraft Kitchens
TX833.5.N48 2003 641.5 C2002-903407-8

10 9 8 7 6 5 4 3 2 1

Text and cover design by: Vicki Hornsby
Cover photography by: Michael Kohn
Printed and bound in Canada
www.randomhouse.ca

Cover: Everyday Easy Lasagna, page 58. Previous page: From an ad for Velveeta, 1938.

The following brands are a part of the Kraft family of tasty and convenient products. In many of the recipes in this book, you'll find shortened references to them. Their full names are given here to help you when you shop:

BAKER'S Semi-Sweet Baking Chocolate
BAKER'S Semi-Sweet Chocolate Chunks
BAKER'S Unsweetened Baking
   Chocolate
CHEEZ WHIZ Cheese Dip
COOL WHIP Whipped Topping
HONEY MAID Honey Grahams
JELL-O Chocolate Flavor Instant
   Pudding & Pie Filling
JELL-O Gelatin
JELL-O Pistachio Flavor Instant
   Pudding & Pie Filling
JELL-O Vanilla Flavor Instant
   Pudding & Pie Filling
KRAFT Barbecue Sauce
KRAFT CATALINA Dressing
KRAFT Classic Caesar Dressing
KRAFT Deluxe Macaroni & Cheese
   Dinner
KRAFT Dressing
KRAFT Italian Style Shredded Cheese
KRAFT LIGHT DONE RIGHT Classic
   Caesar Reduced Fat Dressing
KRAFT LIGHT DONE RIGHT Italian
   Reduced Fat Dressing

KRAFT Macaroni & Cheese Dinner
KRAFT Mayo Real Mayonnaise
KRAFT Mexican Style Shredded
   Cheese
KRAFT 100% Grated Parmesan
   Cheese
KRAFT Peppercorn Ranch Dressing
KRAFT Ranch Dressing
KRAFT Shredded Cheddar Cheese
KRAFT Shredded Cheese
KRAFT Shredded Mozzarella Cheese
KRAFT Singles
KRAFT Swiss Cheese
MINUTE White Rice
MIRACLE WHIP LIGHT Dressing
MIRACLE WHIP Salad Dressing
NILLA Wafers
OREO Chocolate Sandwich Cookies
PHILADELPHIA Chive & Onion Cream
   Cheese Spread
PHILADELPHIA Cream Cheese
PHILADELPHIA Cream Cheese
   Spread
PHILADELPHIA Light Cream Cheese
   Spread

PHILADELPHIA Light Roasted Garlic
   Cream Cheese Spread
PHILADELPHIA Pineapple Cream
   Cheese Spread
PHILADELPHIA Strawberry Cream
   Cheese Spread
POST ALPHA-BITS Frosted
   Letter Shaped Oat and Corn Cereal
POST Cocoa PEBBLES Cereal
POST GOLDEN CRISPS Sweetened
   Puffed Wheat Cereal
POST HONEY BUNCHES OF OATS Cereal
POST 100% Bran Cereal
POST Raisin Bran Cereal
POST SPOON SIZE Shredded Wheat
   Cereal
Raspberry FIG NEWTONS Fruit
   Chewy Cookies
RITZ Crackers
SHAKE'N BAKE Seasoned Coating Mix
STOVE TOP Stuffing Mix
STOVE TOP Stuffing Mix for Chicken
VELVEETA Pasteurized Prepared
   Cheese Product
VELVEETA Shells & Cheese Dinner

Contents

From an ad for Ritz Crackers, mid-1950s.

At the Kraft Kitchens

Here are the people who
helped bring you the book
you are holding right now:

Recipe Content Team
Cécile Girard-Hicks, Stephanie Williams, Lorna Roberts, Tracy Sherva,
Michele McAdoo, Susanne Stark

Recipe Development
Karen Didier, Lisa Brandt-Whittington, Marla Goldberg, Maxine Karpel,
Kathleen Mackintosh, Cayla Runka

Recipe Editor
Betty Heinlen

Marketing Team
Maureen Weiss, Gretchen Claus Hickman, Gillian Fripp, Carol Blindauer,
Lori Sugarman

Photography
All photography produced by Michael Kohn, photographer; Sue Henderson,
food stylist; Catherine MacFadyen, prop stylist; Vicki Hornsby, art director;
Ashley Denton, food-styling assistant; Shelagh McAuliffe, photography assistant;
except for that which appears on pages 16, 91, 100, by Gibson and Smith; 19,
by Michael Alberstat; 60, by Edward Pond; and 76, by Andreas Trauttmansdorff.

Dedicated to all of you, your friends and family,
who have shared our recipes at your tables and made them Classics.

Introduction
100 YEARS OF GREAT CLASSIC TASTES

Think back to your childhood and you may realize that many of your fondest recollections are linked to gatherings of relatives and friends – and to the much-loved family standards that drew you to the table on those special occasions. Maybe it was a favorite cheesecake for Dad's birthday or your grandmother's potato salad at an annual summer barbecue? Even as times change, the value of such traditions stays as strong as ever.

For 100 years, Kraft has helped families like yours to create happy memories involving food. When you needed an easier way to prepare a fresh salad we were there with Miracle Whip, mayonnaise and a host of bottled dressings. When you wanted to get lunch and dinner on the table faster, our Deluxe Process Cheese Slices and Macaroni & Cheese Dinner – ground-breaking products in their time – were there for you. So it continues, as we commit ourselves to helping nurture your family's food memories in the years ahead.

New Classics is the direct result of letters, e-mails and phone calls from many of you, telling us about your favorite Kraft recipes: We listened and we learned, and now we've gathered these most requested and popular recipes into one terrific book to share with family and friends. What exactly is a New Classic? It's a time-honored favorite recipe – yours, your mother's or even your grandmother's – made easier than ever to prepare. That's why we're so sure you'll enjoy every one of these dishes, in the cookbook you helped us to create.

In 1905, a charming child enhanced the Jell-O image as a "dainty dessert." Seventy-five years later, the look was a little more informal (opposite) when it came to Kool-Aid and kids.

Modern lines, 1920s style, marked the design of the first Kraft Kitchen. Kraft offers new choices for the cheese tray (below) and a range of handy cheese-based recipes for eager cooks everywhere. By 1943, the mood was enterprising and solidly patriotic – as in this magazine advertisement for Miracle Whip (right).

Our family tree: A century of classic recipes

Just as the chapters of your family's history go on from generation to generation, Kraft's family of brands has its own history, chronicled in an ever-growing legacy of classic recipes.

In 1903, James Lewis Kraft traveled to Chicago, Illinois, in the U.S., from Fort Erie, Ontario, in Canada. With him, he brought $65, a horse-drawn wagon, the ability to work hard, a knowledge of food and marketing and the determination to build a solid business. Over time, his company grew from a one-man operation into the diverse international organization of today.

At about the same time, Jell-O Brand Gelatin, which later joined the Kraft family of products, was designated "America's Most Famous Dessert" and home economists were called upon to provide helpful tips and new uses of this product for enthusiastic consumers. Still as popular today, Jell-O molded desserts and salads have become true North American classics.

By the 1920s, home cooks everywhere wanted more information about Kraft's expanding family of products. And so the Kraft Kitchens were born. Early kitchen work focused on the needs of cooks at that time, resulting in

innovative recipes featuring cheese in its new, packaged form. Classics that everyone clamored for included toasted cheese sandwiches and macaroni and cheese (see page 66).

As our soldiers marched off to World War II, food shortages and rationing shifted the Kraft Kitchens into high gear. We worked hard to develop dependable, pleasing recipes that met ration requirements. By doing so, we enabled families to enjoy favorite dishes at a time when comfort foods were particularly meaningful. (See Ritz Mock Apple Pie, page 111.) One innovative Kraft classic recipe for chocolate cake even used Miracle Whip Salad Dressing in place of oil. (See Heavenly Chocolate Cake, page 119.)

When television hit the airwaves at the end of the 1940s, it provided yet another way for us to

Victory Gardeners!

For fine nutrition, serve a salad every day

Now, when your garden is rich in sun-ripe vegetables, now's the time to serve *salads* often. Those full-flavored vegetables will taste their best in salads. And, just-picked, they're particularly good sources of essential vitamins and minerals. So ... for fine nutrition ... serve a Victory Garden Salad *every day!*

Salad Eaters!

For unequalled flavor, choose the salad dressing millions prefer

No other salad dressing gives you the just-right flavor of famous *Miracle Whip.* For Miracle Whip is an utterly different type of dressing ... it combines the qualities of zesty boiled dressing and fine mayonnaise. Actually, Miracle Whip is the most popular salad dressing ever created!

Miracle Whip Salad Dressing

KRAFT

Sorry! Kraft Mayonnaise is being made only in limited amounts, because of government restrictions. That's why you may not always find it at your dealer's.

The mood was lively in the decades that followed the end of World War II. In 1961, Kraft Barbecue Sauce (right) was a barbecue essential, and salads were better than ever (below) with Good Seasons Salad Dressing Mix.

share food ideas and techniques. Radio cooking shows now made way for televised food specialists, who prepared enticing recipes before viewers' eyes. The power of this new medium was highlighted dramatically with the airing of a Philadelphia Cream Cheese recipe for trendy clam dip: The television spot caused shortages of canned clams in grocery stores along the entire Eastern seaboard of the United States. (See Classic Clam Dip, page 14.)

During the '60s and '70s, the Kraft Kitchens responded to the new demand for time-saving recipes. As more women entered the work force, we devised quicker recipes to put home-cooked family meals on the table with less time and effort. Recipes featuring convenience ingredients, such as Minute White Rice and Cool Whip Whipped Topping, were among these new classics. We also developed speedy kitchen tips – such as softening cream cheese or melting chocolate in a microwave oven – to share with our consumers.

When fitness and health took the spotlight in the

New Kraft Barbecue Sauce simmers real cook-out flavor right into the meat!

When it starts to simmer, the flavor really speaks up. This is the barbecue sauce that gives you the flavor you cook outdoors to get. The Kraft cooks made it that way—with nineteen herbs and spices. And once it's on the fire, those simmering spice flavors seep right in and keep the meat juicy. Try new Kraft Barbecue Sauce in your kitchen, too; cooks who do say that it brings its real cook-out flavor right indoors—and what could be better than that?

'80s and '90s, many of Kraft's favorite recipes were revised to accommodate the desire for wider dietary choice. And reduced-calorie, sugar-free or reduced-fat versions of food favorites such as Kraft Dressings and Kraft cheese were introduced.

Our families today: The dawn of a new century

The twenty-first century is here, and as *New Classics* illustrates, Kraft is already attuned to your family's present needs. Busy lifestyles have gotten busier, and so our quick classic recipes take even less time than before. Because a generation raised on salsa craves intense flavors, we've updated familiar recipes with zesty new ingredients, as well.

Despite all the changes, one classic concept stays the same – the importance of gathering around a table with loved ones to share delicious home cooking. So open this book and create some memorable moments of your very own to enjoy with those you hold dear. And remember to keep in touch with us. Thanks to you, tomorrow's newest classic may be just around the corner.

Brand new in the 1960s – revolutionary Cool Whip Whipped Topping (left); and in the 1970s, Kraft Singles made their mark (below).

MAKING YOUR EVERYDAY COOKING EASIER

**HOW WE DEMYSTIFY
EVERYDAY COOKING**

It's easiest for us to explain the process by comparing the method we once used to explain a recipe (we'll use a stir-fry here) with the way we approach the same dish today.

Twenty years ago, our method of putting together a chicken stir-fry was a traditional one that looked pretty much like this:

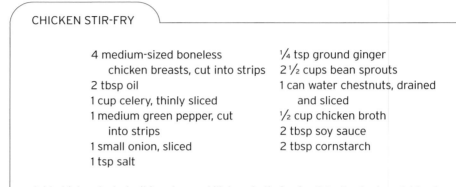

CHICKEN STIR-FRY

4 medium-sized boneless
  chicken breasts, cut into strips
2 tbsp oil
1 cup celery, thinly sliced
1 medium green pepper, cut
  into strips
1 small onion, sliced
1 tsp salt

¼ tsp ground ginger
2 ½ cups bean sprouts
1 can water chestnuts, drained
  and sliced
½ cup chicken broth
2 tbsp soy sauce
2 tbsp cornstarch

Add chicken to hot oil in a large skillet and stir-fry for 2 to 3 minutes. Add celery, green pepper, onion, salt and ginger; stir-fry until vegetables are tender-crisp. Add bean sprouts, water chestnuts and chicken broth. Combine soy sauce and cornstarch; mix until smooth. Gradually stir soy mixture into chicken-broth mixture and cook, stirring constantly, until sauce is thickened. Serve over prepared rice. Serves 4.

When we thought about it, that traditional stir-fry seemed like a lot of work. It was, after all, just some meat, vegetables and sauce, served over rice.

So we began to undo the process, replacing 5 separate measured ingredients (and the inescapable challenge of keeping the cornstarch from lumping) with a splash of flavorful salad dressing as the foundation of our sauce. A few minor ingredients – like those water chestnuts – got lost along the way and we focused on the easy-to-grasp rules of thumb that would always work: a pound of meat for 4 people and a handful of each of the vegetables per person. We'd leave it up to you to cover a pan or leave it uncovered (although if it was important to do one or the other, we'd be sure to tell you).

And suddenly our stir-fry wasn't so complicated. In fact, with that stir-fry we were able to take the whole process down to 3 simple steps: starting the meat on its own; adding vegetables to the skillet partway through; then finishing the dish with some dressing to make the sauce.

Here's the result. With our recipes we utilize easy-to-follow 4-color grids – which show 4 tasty combinations of popular meat, vegetables and flavorings – to get you started. After you've practiced our approach it really becomes exciting, as you use the same simple process to mix and match ingredients to perfectly satisfy your own family's tastes.

THE SIMPLE STIR-FRY

Just follow our 3 simple steps:

1 STIR-FRY sliced **meat** (1 lb should do it for 4) with a bit of Kraft **dressing** for 10 minutes.

2 ADD sliced **veggies** (a handful per person) and cook 10 minutes more.

3 STIR in an additional ½ cup dressing to make a sauce. Serve over prepared rice.

And use the ingredients you have on hand …

What **meat** do you feel like?	What **veggies** are on hand?	Add a **dressing**
chicken breast	cauliflower, peppers, broccoli	sun-dried tomato
beef sirloin	celery, carrots	Italian
pork loin	red cabbage, apples, onions	Catalina
meatless	carrots, broccoli, onions, cauliflower	Italian

We're Here to Help You

If you need help, just give us a call or send an e-mail.

Not every cookbook comes with a helpline, but ours does. Here in the Kraft Kitchens we listen to you and we're here to help with your cooking needs. Monday to Friday, 9 a.m. to 9 p.m. EST, you can call our helpline.

Our websites also provide additional classic recipes, all sorts of terrific dinner solutions, cooking tips and holiday ideas.

Whatever the method, we hope you will be in touch. We'd love to hear from you, whenever you have the time.

IN CANADA
HELPLINE
1-800-567-KRAFT
(9 a.m. to 9 p.m. EST,
Monday to Friday)
E-MAIL
kraftkitchens@kraft.com
WEBSITE

kraftcanada.com

IN THE UNITED STATES
HELPLINE
1-877-572-3843 (toll-free)
(9 a.m. to 9 p.m. EST,
Monday to Friday)
E-MAIL
classics@kraftfoods.com
WEBSITE

kraftfoods.com

First impressions should always be memorable, especially when they involve the food you put on your table. That welcome snack at the end of a busy afternoon, the flavorful dish that marks the start of a family dinner or the irresistible plate of goodies set out for an evening at home doesn't have to be complicated or time-consuming to prepare. It simply has to taste delicious. If it looks appealing

Starters & Soups

and its smells are enticing even better, of course – because anticipation is such a big part of the pleasure. And that's the focus of every easy Kraft Kitchens recipe you'll find in the pages that follow. We've taken many of your favorite snack mixes, savory finger foods, luscious dips and heartwarming soups, featuring time-tested combinations of ingredients we know you love, and we've made them easier and better tasting than ever before. Which is why we're sure you're going to enjoy every one of these recipes and why we think of them as true New Classics.

Previous page: From an ad for Velveeta, 1960.

THE ORIGINAL MUNCH MIX

Just follow our 3 simple steps:

1 PLACE 4 cups Post Spoon Size Shredded Wheat Cereal, 2 cups popped popcorn, 1 cup small pretzels and 1 cup mixed nuts or peanuts in 15- x 10- x 1-inch baking pan. Sprinkle evenly with 1 envelope Italian salad dressing mix.

2 MIX ¼ cup butter or margarine, melted, 2 tablespoons Worcestershire sauce and ¼ teaspoon garlic powder. Drizzle evenly over cereal mixture; stir to coat.

3 BAKE at 300°F for 30–35 minutes or until crisp, stirring halfway through baking time. Cool. Store in tightly covered container up to 1 week.

>> KRAFT KITCHENS TIP
After Munch Mix has cooled, have the kids spoon 2-cup portions into small plastic bags and tie with colorful holiday ribbons. Give these gifts to the mailman, crossing guard or anyone else who makes a difference in your life.

CRUNCHY PARMESAN POPCORN

Just follow our 3 simple steps:

1 MIX 12 cups hot, unsalted popped popcorn (⅓ cup, unpopped) with ⅓ cup *each* butter or margarine and grated Parmesan cheese; toss lightly until well coated.

2 SPREAD in single layer on baking sheet.

3 BAKE at 375°F for 5–7 minutes or until golden brown.

10-MINUTE APPETIZER DIPS

>> TRY THIS, TOO
For a great substitute, use Philadelphia Light Cream Cheese Spread and Miracle Whip Light.

>> CLASSIC CLAM DIP
Mix 1 can (6-½ oz) minced clams, 1 package (8 oz) Philadelphia Cream Cheese, softened, 2 teaspoons lemon juice, 1-½ teaspoons Worcestershire sauce and ¼ teaspoon garlic salt. Serve with potato chips.

Just follow our 3 simple steps:

1 MIX 1 package (8 oz) Philadelphia Cream Cheese, softened, with ½ cup Miracle Whip. Spread mixture on pie plate or serving platter.

2 LAYER sliced/chopped **toppings** on base.

3 SPRINKLE with **Kraft Shredded Cheese**. Serve with pita bread, crackers, tortilla chips and fresh veggies.

And use the ingredients you have on hand …

What **toppings** do you have on hand?	And finish with **Kraft Shredded Cheese**
salsa, tomatoes, shredded lettuce	Mexican Style
tomatoes, cucumbers, black olives	Mozzarella
pesto, artichokes, grilled eggplant and peppers	Italian Style
pasta or pizza sauce, pepperoni, peppers	Italian Style

HOT DIPS

SWISS ALMOND DIP

Just follow our 2 simple steps:

1 MIX in pie plate or ovenproof serving dish, 1 package (8 oz) cream cheese, softened, 1-½ cups shredded Kraft Swiss Cheese, ⅓ cup *each* mayonnaise and chopped green onions.

2 BAKE at 350°F for 15 minutes, stirring once during baking. Top with slivered almonds. Serve warm with pita crisps, baguette slices, broccoli, cauliflower and asparagus.

ARTICHOKE DIP

Just follow our 2 simple steps:

1 MIX in a pie plate or ovenproof dish, 1 cup *each* mayonnaise and Kraft 100% Grated Parmesan Cheese, with 1 can (14 oz) artichoke hearts, drained and chopped.

2 BAKE at 350°F for 15 minutes or until dip is hot and bubbly. Serve with assorted dippers such as vegetables and crackers.

CHILI-CHEESE DIP

Just follow our 3 simple steps:

1 SPREAD 1 package (8 oz) cream cheese, softened, on bottom of microwavable pie plate.

2 TOP with 1 can (15 oz) chili; sprinkle with shredded Cheddar cheese.

3 MICROWAVE on HIGH 3 minutes or until thoroughly heated. Serve warm with tortilla chips.

>> TRY THIS, TOO

Sprinkle Chili-Cheese Dip with ½ cup *each* chopped onion and chopped green pepper before topping with chili and cheese.

>> VELVEETA SALSA DIP

Cube 1 lb Velveeta and mix with 1 cup salsa in a microwavable bowl. Microwave on HIGH for 5 minutes or until melted, stirring after 2 minutes.

FRESH TOMATO-AND-HERB BRUSCHETTA

>> KRAFT KITCHENS TIP
To seed tomatoes, cut in half crosswise and gently squeeze out seeds over sink or use a spoon to scoop out seeds.

Just follow our 2 simple steps:
1 SLICE French bread into thick slices and grill until golden.
2 MIX 4 large tomatoes, seeded and chopped, several spoonfuls of sun-dried tomato vinaigrette dressing and a handful of shredded Italian-style cheese in small bowl. Serve tomato mixture with grilled bread.

DEVILED EGGS

Just follow our 3 simple steps:
1 CUT 6 hard-cooked eggs in half lengthwise; remove yolks.
2 MIX yolks with ⅓ cup Miracle Whip.
3 SPOON yolk mixture into egg whites; sprinkle with paprika.

SHAKE'N BAKE CHICKEN FINGERS

Just follow our 2 simple steps:
1 CUT 5-6 boneless, skinless chicken breasts into strips. Coat with Shake'N Bake Original Coating Mix as directed on package.
2 BAKE at 400°F for 10 minutes or until cooked through. Serve with barbecue sauce, salsa or honey as a dip.

4 WAYS WITH NACHOS

Just follow our 3 simple steps:

1 PLACE a layer of **tortilla chips** or **crackers** in baking dish.

2 MIX 2 cups **shredded cheese** and **add-ins** in bowl; spread half evenly over nachos. Repeat layers, ending with topping layer.

3 BAKE at 400°F for 8–10 minutes or until cheese melts.

And use the ingredients you have on hand …

What **tortilla chips** or **crackers** do you want?	Use this **shredded cheese**	Try these **add-ins**
blue tortilla chips	Mexican-style	diced cooked chicken, tomatoes and jalapeño peppers
tortilla chips, triangular	Cheddar	diced tomatoes, frozen corn, kidney beans and chili powder
whole-wheat crackers	Italian-style	diced tomatoes, zucchini, black olives and dash of oregano
snack crackers	mozzarella	strips of pepper, garlic powder and dash of oregano

MANHATTAN MEATBALLS

>> **KRAFT KITCHENS TIP**
Meatballs cook evenly
when they are all the same
size. Use a small ice-cream
scoop or scant ¼ cup
measuring cup to portion
even amounts of meat.

Just follow our 3 simple steps:

1 MIX 2 lb ground **meat**, 1 cup dry seasoned bread crumbs and 2 eggs. Shape into 1-inch meatballs, placing on foil-lined 15- x 10- x 1-inch baking pan.

2 MIX 1 cup Kraft Original Barbecue Sauce, 1 jar (12 oz) **jelly or preserves** and a spoonful of **seasoning**. Pour over meatballs.

3 BAKE at 375°F for 40 minutes, stirring halfway through cooking.

And use the ingredients you have on hand …

What ground **meat** do you feel like?	Which **jelly or preserves** do you have on hand?	And now for the **seasoning**
turkey	peach preserves	ground ginger
beef	grape jelly	black pepper
pork	apricot preserves	soy sauce
pork sausage	orange marmalade	hot pepper flakes

MANHATTAN CLAM CHOWDER

Just follow our 3 simple steps:
1 DRAIN 2 cans (6-½ oz *each*) minced clams, reserving liquid. Add enough water to reserved liquid to measure 3 cups.
2 SIMMER clam juice/water mixture, 1 can (16 oz) undrained diced tomatoes, ½ cup *each* chopped onion and carrot, 2 potatoes, peeled and cubed, and ½ teaspoon dried thyme in large covered saucepan for 30 minutes.
3 REMOVE from heat and mash vegetables slightly to thicken broth. Stir in minced clams. Heat thoroughly. Season to taste with salt and pepper.

NEW ENGLAND CLAM CHOWDER

Just follow our 3 simple steps:
1 COOK 4 slices bacon in medium saucepan until crisp; drain and set aside, reserving 2 tablespoons bacon drippings.
2 SAUTÉ 2 potatoes, peeled and cubed, and ¼ cup *each* chopped carrot, onion and celery in reserved bacon drippings until tender.
3 STIR in 1 tub (8 oz) cream cheese spread, 2 cans (6-½ oz *each*) minced clams with juice, cooked bacon, 2 cups milk and 1 cup water. Simmer 15-20 minutes.

SMOOTH & CREAMY VEGETABLE SOUPS

>> KRAFT KITCHENS TIP
For a healthful alternative
to traditional cream
soups, we've thickened
our version with a puree
of rice and vegetables
in place of heavy cream.

Just follow our 3 simple steps:

1 MIX 1 *each* onion, carrot and celery stalk, chopped, in large pot with 2 cans (10-½ oz *each*) condensed chicken broth and 3 cans water. Bring to boil. Cook 5-10 minutes or until tender.
2 ADD 4 cups chopped **veggies**, ½ cup uncooked Minute White Rice, salt and pepper to taste and 1-2 teaspoons **spices**. Cook on medium heat 10-15 minutes or until veggies are tender. Pour in 1 can milk.
3 PURÉE soup in batches, in a blender or food processor, return to pot and gently heat on low until warm.

And use the ingredients you have on hand …

What **veggies** do you feel like?	Now for the **spices**
broccoli	chili powder
cauliflower	curry powder
carrots	ground ginger
peeled butternut squash	ground nutmeg

Creamy Cauliflower Soup

FRENCH ONION SOUP

Just follow our 3 simple steps:
1 PLACE 3 large Spanish onions, sliced, 1 can (10-½ oz) condensed beef broth, 1 can water and 1 bay leaf in large pot. Bring to a boil, reduce heat and simmer 25 minutes.
2 REMOVE bay leaf and divide into 6 ovenproof bowls, topping each bowl with slice of toasted French bread.
3 COMBINE shredded Swiss, mozzarella and Parmesan cheese. Sprinkle each bowl with a handful of cheese. Broil 5-10 minutes or until cheese melts.

CHEESY BROCCOLI SOUP

Just follow our 3 simple steps:
1 COOK 1 large bunch broccoli, chopped, and 2 carrots, chopped, in saucepan with 1 can (10-½ oz) condensed chicken broth and 1 can water until tender. Let cool 10 minutes.
2 POUR into blender; cover. Process until smooth; return to saucepan.
3 WHISK in ½ cup milk and 1 cup Cheez Whiz on low heat. Do not allow to boil.

A century is a long time, and over the past 100 years we've made an interesting and diverse assortment of delicious salads and other vegetable dishes. In many instances, their styles directly reflect the time of their invention. Some of these mealtime standards have been with us for years and years, and yet the best of them still seem as fresh and right as they were the very first time they

Salads & Sides

were served. All they need is a minor touch or two to make them seem an absolutely perfect fit for modern-day sensibilities and tastes. We love the names of them – Waldorf and Cobb salads, for example, and old-fashioned Corn Pudding. We also love the memories they evoke, of family reunions, community suppers, school picnics or summertime company celebrations. We think you'll be more than happy to remember such old favorites, especially when you discover that these recipes make them easier and better-tasting than they've ever been before.

Previous page: From an ad for Good Seasons Salad Dressing, 1960.

CREATE A COLESLAW

Just follow our 2 simple steps:
1 POUR 1 package shredded-coleslaw mix into large bowl.
2 TOSS with creamy coleslaw dressing and an add-in or two, if you like.

Choose from these add-ins:

1 can (11 oz) of mandarin-orange segments, drained; chopped red and green apples; handful of bacon bits; horseradish; nuts and raisins; pickle relish; shredded carrot; 1 cup crushed pineapple; spoonful of dill; spoonful of mustard.

TANGY BROCCOLI SALAD

Just follow our 2 simple steps:
1 MIX 1 cup Miracle Whip or Miracle Whip Light and 2 tablespoons *each* sugar and vinegar in large bowl.
2 ADD 1 medium bunch broccoli, cut into florets (about 6 cups), a handful of bacon bits and ½ medium red onion, chopped. Cover. Refrigerate until ready to serve.

>> INSIDE A CLASSIC
In the 1930s, Kraft introduced Miracle Whip Salad Dressing – a product that combined the best features of mayonnaise and old-fashioned boiled dressing. For the first time, salads began to be served regularly in homes throughout North America.

WALDORF SALAD

>> KRAFT KITCHENS TIP
For optimum flavor, use
tart apples, such as Granny
Smiths, in this classic
Waldorf Salad recipe.

Toss 3 cups coarsely chopped apples, 1 cup sliced celery and ½ cup *each* Kraft Mayo and coarsely chopped walnuts. Cover. Refrigerate until ready to serve. Serve in lettuce-lined bowl, if desired.

Also try one of these add-ins:

Chopped cooked chicken or turkey; chopped dates; halved seedless green grapes; miniature marshmallows; raisins or toasted coconut.

WATERGATE SALAD

Just follow our 3 simple steps:

1 MIX 1 package (4-serving size) Jell-O Pistachio Flavor Instant Pudding & Pie Filling, 1 can (20 oz) crushed pineapple with juice, 1 cup miniature marshmallows and ½ cup chopped pecans in large bowl until well blended.
2 ADD 2 cups thawed whipped topping; stir gently. Cover. Refrigerate 1 hour or until ready to serve.
3 TOP with additional whipped topping and sliced strawberries just before serving, if desired.

5-CUP SALAD

Just follow our 2 simple steps:
1 TOSS 1 can (11 oz) mandarin orange segments, drained, 1 cup *each* pineapple chunks, coconut, miniature marshmallows and sour cream. Cover.
2 REFRIGERATE several hours or until chilled.

COBB SALAD

Just follow our 3 simple steps:
1 ARRANGE 6 cups torn mixed salad greens, 2 cups chopped deli turkey slices, 2 tomatoes, chopped, 2 hard-cooked eggs, chopped, and 1 avocado, peeled and chopped, on large serving platter.
2 SPRINKLE 6 slices bacon, crisply cooked and crumbled, and 2 cups shredded Cheddar cheese over top.
3 DRIZZLE with French dressing. Sprinkle with crumbled blue cheese, if desired.

>> TRY THIS, TOO Cobb Salad is also great with ranch dressing.

>> KRAFT KITCHENS TIP
For a more interesting texture, try toasting the coconut in 5-Cup Salad.

Thinly spread coconut on baking sheet. Bake at 350°F for 7-12 minutes, stirring occasionally, until lightly browned.

POTATO SALAD

Just follow our 3 simple steps:

1 MIX ¾ cup **dressing** and a spoonful of **seasonings** in large bowl.

2 ADD 6 cups cubed cooked potatoes (about 2 lb) and chopped **add-ins** (a handful of *each* should do it); mix lightly. Cover.

3 REFRIGERATE several hours or until chilled.

And use the ingredients you have on hand …

What **dressing** do you feel like?	Try these **seasonings**	And now for the **add-ins**
Miracle Whip or mayonnaise	Dijon mustard	celery, hard-cooked eggs and sweet pickle relish
sour cream	chopped fresh dill	cucumber, hard-cooked eggs and red onion
Italian	minced garlic	feta cheese, green pepper and red onion
ranch	chopped cilantro	corn, red or green pepper and canned green chilies

Potato Salad with Celery, Hard-Cooked Eggs and Sweet Pickle Relish

CLASSIC GREEK SALAD

Just follow our 2 simple steps:
1 MIX 3 tomatoes, chopped, 1 cucumber, sliced, and ½ cup *each* thinly sliced red onion and whole ripe Kalamata olives in large bowl.
2 TOSS with 1 cup crumbled feta cheese and ½ cup Greek vinaigrette dressing.

TACO SALAD

Just follow our 3 simple steps:
1 BROWN 1 lb ground beef; drain. Add 1 package (1-¼ oz) taco-seasoning mix; prepare as directed on package.
2 PLACE shredded iceberg lettuce in large serving bowl; cover with layers of ground beef mixture, Kraft Shredded Cheddar Cheese and tomato wedges.
3 TOP with pitted black olives, crushed tortilla chips, salsa and sour cream.

>> **TRY THIS, TOO**
Serve prepared Greek Salad ingredients over torn romaine or iceberg lettuce. Or serve with toasted pita bread wedges.

You can also substitute Italian reduced-fat dressing for Greek vinaigrette dressing in this Greek Salad.

CAESAR SALAD

>> **TRY THIS, TOO**
You can also substitute
Kraft Caesar Reduced Fat
Dressing for regular
dressing in this Caesar
Salad.

TOSS 8 cups torn romaine lettuce, 1 cup seasoned croutons and ½ cup *each* shredded Parmesan cheese and Kraft Caesar Dressing in large salad bowl. Serve immediately.

SPINACH SALAD

>> **CHICKEN CAESAR SALAD**
Toss 2 cups cooked chicken
strips with other salad
ingredients. Add additional
dressing, if desired.

Just follow our 3 simple steps:
1 TOSS 2 packages (10 oz *each*) fresh baby spinach in large bowl with ½ small red onion, sliced, 4 hard-cooked eggs, chopped, and 1 cup sliced fresh mushrooms.
2 MICROWAVE ½ cup Italian dressing in microwavable measuring cup on HIGH for 20 seconds. Drizzle over salad; toss lightly.
3 SPRINKLE with bacon bits.

EVERYDAY EASY RICE SALADS

Just follow our 3 simple steps:

1 TOSS 4 cups cooked Minute White Rice with a few handfuls of chopped **veggies/fruit**.

2 MIX 1 cup Miracle Whip or Miracle Whip Light with **juice/peel** and **seasonings**.

3 ADD to rice mixture; toss to coat. Serve immediately or cover and refrigerate until ready to serve.

And use the ingredients you have on hand …

What **veggies/fruit** are on hand?	And now for the **juice/peel**	Finish it off with a **seasoning**
peppers, green onions and 1 can (11 oz) mandarin-orange segments, drained	1/2 cup orange juice	dash ground ginger
mango and red onion	juice and grated peel of 1 lime	spoonful soy sauce
cooked asparagus spears and cherry tomatoes	juice and grated peel of 1 lemon	spoonful Dijon mustard and chopped fresh parsley
apples and celery	1 cup apple juice	dash curry powder

EASY ROASTED VEGETABLES

Just follow our 3 simple steps:
1 PLACE any combination of cut-up vegetables, such as potatoes, carrots, onions, Brussels sprouts or parsnips, in 9- x 13-inch baking dish.
2 POUR sun-dried tomato vinaigrette dressing over vegetables; toss to coat.
3 BAKE at 400°F for 1 hour or until vegetables are tender, stirring occasionally.

BROCCOLI-RICE CASSEROLE

Just follow our 3 simple steps:
1 COOK ½ cup chopped onion in 1 tablespoon butter or margarine in large skillet until tender, stirring frequently.
2 ADD 2 cups *each* cooked Minute White Rice and small broccoli florets, 1 can (10-¾ oz) condensed cream of mushroom soup and 1 cup Cheez Whiz; mix well. Spoon into 1-½-qt baking dish; sprinkle with ½ cup fresh bread cubes.
3 BAKE at 350°F for 30-35 minutes or until thoroughly heated.

AU GRATIN POTATOES

1 tub (8 oz) Philadelphia Cream Cheese Spread
2 tablespoons flour
2 cups milk
3 cups shredded sharp Cheddar cheese, divided
6 medium potatoes (about 2 lb) peeled, very thinly sliced
1 medium onion, thinly sliced

1 MIX cream cheese spread, flour and milk with wire whisk in medium saucepan until well blended. Cook on medium heat until cream cheese spread is melted and mixture is hot and bubbly, stirring frequently.
2 STIR in 2 cups of the Cheddar cheese; cook until completely melted, stirring frequently. Spread thin layer of cheese sauce on bottom of greased 9- x 13-inch baking dish. Layer potatoes, onion and cheese sauce alternately in baking dish. Season with salt and pepper; cover.
3 BAKE at 400°F for 1 hour or until potatoes are tender. Uncover; sprinkle with remaining 1 cup shredded Cheddar cheese. Bake an additional 5 minutes or until cheese is melted. *Serves 8.*

>> **TRY THIS, TOO**
Philadelphia Light Cream Cheese Spread makes a great substitute in these au gratin potatoes.

>> **FLAVORED MASHED POTATOES**
Stir ½ cup (half 8-oz tub) Philadelphia Chive & Onion or Light Roasted Garlic Cream Cheese Spread into 6 cups hot mashed potatoes until cream cheese spread is completely melted.

CORN PUDDING

>> **TRY THIS, TOO**
A delicious corn pudding can also be made by substituting 1 package (8-½ oz) corn-muffin mix for the baking mix, cornmeal and sugar.

1 can (15-¼ oz) whole kernel corn, drained
1 can (14-¾ oz) cream-style corn
1 cup sour cream
1 cup buttermilk baking mix
½ cup cornmeal
⅓ cup sugar
3 eggs, slightly beaten
¼ cup margarine or butter, melted

1 MIX all ingredients until well blended.
2 POUR mixture into greased 9- x 13-inch baking dish.
3 BAKE at 375°F for 35–40 minutes, until edges are golden brown. *Serves 16.*

CLASSIC GREEN BEAN CASSEROLE

Just follow our 3 simple steps:
1 MIX 3 packages (9 oz *each*) French-cut green beans, thawed and drained, with 1 can (10-¾ oz) condensed cream of mushroom soup, 1 cup Cheez Whiz and half of 1 can (2.8 oz) of French-fried onions in 1-½-qt baking dish.
2 BAKE at 350°F for 30 minutes.
3 TOP with remaining French-fried onions. Bake an additional 5 minutes.

PARMESAN GARLIC BREAD 4 WAYS

Just follow our 3 simple steps:

1 MIX 1 cup mayonnaise and ½ cup *each* shredded mozzarella cheese and grated Parmesan cheese.

2 ADD 1 garlic clove, minced; mix well. Spread evenly over toasted French baguette slices.

3 BAKE at 350°F for 5-7 minutes or until cheese mixture is melted. Serve immediately.

Parmesan Garlic Bread is also terrific in the following ways:

BACON-AND-ONION GARLIC BREAD

Prepare as directed, adding bacon bits and 2 green onions, sliced, to mayonnaise mixture and substituting toasted pumpernickel bread for toasted baguette slices.

BETTA BRUSCHETTA

Prepare as directed, adding chopped tomato and chopped red onion to mayonnaise mixture and substituting toasted Kaiser rolls, halved, for toasted baguette slices.

EXTRA-CHEESY GARLIC BREAD

Prepare as directed, substituting shredded Italian-style cheese for mozzarella cheese and toasted rye bread for toasted baguette slices.

5-INGREDIENT CHEDDAR BISCUITS

Just follow our 3 simple steps:

1 MIX 2 cups flour and 1 tablespoon baking powder. Cut in 1 tub (8 oz) cream cheese spread with 2 knives, a food processor or your hands to form a crumbly mixture.

2 STIR in ½ cup milk and a handful of shredded Cheddar cheese, if desired, stirring until dough holds together.

3 PAT dough ¾-inch thick on floured counter. Cut 10-12 biscuits with the top of a glass or with a cookie cutter. Place on baking sheet and bake at 425°F for 12-15 minutes.

At the heart of every pleasing meal, there's sure to be a main dish that performs on more than just one level. First, of course, it satisfies hunger. But a good main dish should also please the eye, tantalize with mouthwatering aromas and bring real pleasure to the taste buds. And did we forget to say that it should also be simple to make? Over the years, the Kraft Kitchens have learned a lot about

Main Dishes

what works best in kitchens just like yours. The great-tasting main dishes described in the pages that follow include many family favorites – frequently brought up-to-date with today's most popular ingredients and terrific time-saving techniques. Whether you're in the mood for an all-in-one skillet supper, a hearty casserole, the perfect freshly made sandwich, endlessly versatile chicken or even fish and chips, we're here with the perfect solution. You're about to discover those family classics all over again, and maybe even like them more than before.

Previous page: From a Kraft ad, 1985.

ITALIAN PASTA BAKE

1 lb lean ground beef or ground turkey
8 oz (about 3 cups) pasta, cooked and drained
1 jar (28 oz) spaghetti sauce
¾ cup Kraft 100% Grated Parmesan Cheese
2 cups shredded mozzarella cheese

1 BROWN meat in large skillet; drain. Stir in pasta, sauce and ½ cup of the Parmesan cheese.
2 SPOON into 9- x 13-inch baking dish; top with mozzarella cheese and remaining ¼ cup Parmesan cheese.
3 BAKE at 375°F for 20 minutes. *Serves 6.*

>> **VEGETABLE PASTA BAKE**
Prepare as directed, omitting ground meat and stirring in 1 package (16 oz) frozen mixed vegetables, thawed, with pasta.

EVERYDAY EASY LASAGNAS

>> **KRAFT KITCHENS TIP**
Be sure to completely cover
your lasagna noodles with
sauce before baking.

Just follow our 3 simple steps:

1 BROWN **meat** and chopped **veggies** in a bit of oil in large skillet.

2 STIR in **sauce** and a couple handfuls of Kraft Shredded Mozzarella Cheese.

3 LAYER with oven-ready (no-boil) lasagna noodles in 9- x 13-inch baking dish; sprinkle with more cheese. Cover with foil and bake at 400°F for 30 minutes.

And use the ingredients you have on hand …

What **meat** do you feel like?	Add the **veggies**	And now for the **sauce**
1 lb boneless, skinless chicken strips	peppers	3 cups salsa and 1 cup water
1 lb ground beef	onions	3 cups spaghetti sauce and 1 cup water
2 handfuls sliced pepperoni	peppers	3 cups spaghetti sauce and 1 cup water
meatless	onions and mushrooms	2 cans (10-3/4 oz *each*) condensed cream of mushroom soup and 2 cans water

Everyday Easy Pepperoni Lasagna

VELVEETA ONE-PAN PLEASERS

Just follow our 3 simple steps:

1 BROWN **meat** (1 lb should do it for 4) in large skillet.

2 ADD **sauce** and 2 cups water. Bring to boil. Stir in 2 cups elbow macaroni or tiny shell pasta. Reduce heat to medium–low; cover with tight-fitting lid. Simmer 10-12 minutes or until pasta is tender.

3 ADD ¾ lb (12 oz) Velveeta, cut up, a few handfuls of **veggies** and dash of **seasonings**; cook until vegetables are heated. Let stand 5 minutes.

And use the ingredients you have on hand …

>> TRY THIS, TOO
Substitute 1 package (14 oz) Velveeta Shells & Cheese for Velveeta and pasta. Prepare as directed, reducing water to 1-½ cups and increasing simmering time to 15 minutes.

What **meat** do you feel like?	What **sauce** do you have on hand?	Try these **veggies** and **seasonings**
boneless, skinless chicken breasts, cut up	1 can (10-3/4 oz) condensed cream of chicken soup	chopped broccoli, garlic powder
ground beef	1-1/2 cups salsa	corn, ground cumin
1 package (10 oz) smoked ham, chopped	1 can (10-3/4 oz) condensed cream of mushroom soup	mixed vegetable blend, Dijon mustard
1 can (6 oz) tuna, drained and flaked*	1 can (10-3/4 oz) condensed cream of celery soup	peas, Italian seasoning

*add with sauce and water

FAMILY-FAVORITE TUNA CASSEROLES

Just follow our 3 simple steps:

1 PLACE 2 cups **pasta** and 4 cups water in skillet; stir. Cook on high heat for 8–12 minutes or until pasta is tender, adding **veggies** (a few handfuls per person should do it) during final few minutes of pasta-cooking time.

2 REDUCE heat to medium. Stir in 1 can (10 -¾ oz) condensed cream of mushroom soup, 1 can (6 oz) tuna, drained and flaked, and a few handfuls of **Kraft Shredded Cheese**.

3 TOP with a few more handfuls of cheese; cover. Cook an additional 2 minutes or until cheese is melted.

And use the ingredients you have on hand …

What **pasta** do you feel like?	Try these **veggies**	Add this **Kraft Shredded Cheese**
elbow macaroni	peas, sliced celery	Cheddar
rotini	broccoli florets	Italian Style
fusilli	peas, sliced carrots	Cheddar
small shells	corn	Mexican Style

Tuna Casserole with Broccoli

15-MINUTE RICE DINNERS

Just follow our 3 simple steps:

1 COOK **meat** in a little oil in large covered skillet for about 10 minutes. Additional time will be required for chicken and less time for ham.

2 ADD **liquid** and 2 cups uncooked Minute White Rice (enough to serve 4). Bring to boil.

3 STIR in **add-ins**; cover. Let stand 5 minutes before serving.

And use the ingredients you have on hand …

>> SHARING OUR EXPERIENCES
Whenever I have leftover meat, rice or vegetables, I make a great lunch the next day. Fill large warmed flour tortillas with a few spoonfuls of warmed-up leftovers, roll and serve.
—Michele, Kraft Kitchens

What **meat** do you feel like?	Choose a **liquid** for sauce and flavor	Finish it with **add-ins**
4 boneless, skinless chicken breast halves	1 can (10-3/4 oz) condensed cream of chicken soup and 1 can water	salt and pepper
1 lb ground beef	1 cup *each* salsa and water	shredded Cheddar cheese, corn
2 cups chopped cooked ham	1 can (14 oz) pineapple tidbits and 1 can water	chopped peppers
6 boneless chicken thighs	1 can (10-3/4 oz) condensed cream of chicken soup and 1 can water	1 package (16 oz) frozen stir-fry veggies (thawed), a few spoonfuls soy sauce

3-CHEESE BAKED MACARONI & CHEESE

Just follow our 3 simple steps:

1 PREPARE 1 package (14 oz) Kraft Deluxe Macaroni & Cheese Dinner as directed on package. Stir in ½ cup shredded mozzarella cheese and 1 cup milk.

2 SPOON into greased 1-½-qt casserole. Sprinkle with 1 cup shredded Cheddar cheese.

3 BAKE at 375°F for 20 minutes or until thoroughly heated.

3-Cheese Baked Macaroni & Cheese is also terrific in the following ways:

HAM-AND-BROCCOLI BAKED MACARONI & CHEESE
Prepare macaroni & cheese mixture as directed, stirring in a couple hand-fuls *each* chopped ham and frozen chopped broccoli, thawed, and a spoon-ful Dijon mustard with mozzarella cheese.

TACO MAC SQUARES
Prepare macaroni & cheese mixture as directed. Spoon into 8-inch square baking dish. Cook and season 1 lb lean ground beef with 1 package (1-¼ oz) taco-seasoning mix as directed on package. Spoon over mixture; sprinkle with Cheddar cheese. Bake as directed.

>> **KRAFT KITCHENS TIP** To make this casserole extra special, sprinkle ½ cup crushed buttery crackers over casserole before baking.

SIMPLE SPAGHETTI AND MEATBALLS

Just follow our 2 simple steps:
1 COOK spaghetti as directed on package; drain. Meanwhile, mix 1 jar (26 oz) spaghetti sauce and prepared Master Meatballs (see below; use about 4–5 meatballs per serving) in large skillet; cook on medium-high until thoroughly heated, stirring occasionally.
2 PLACE cooked spaghetti in serving bowl; top with sauce mixture. Sprinkle with grated Parmesan cheese.

>> KRAFT KITCHENS TIP
You can freeze cooked meatballs with prepared sauce in a sealable plastic freezer bag.

MASTER MEATBALLS

Just follow our 3 simple steps:
1 MIX 1 lb extra-lean ground beef with ½ cup *each* dry bread crumbs and barbecue sauce, 1 egg and a few spoonfuls of grated Parmesan cheese until well blended.
2 ROLL into 1-inch balls; place in 15- x 10- x 1-inch baking pan.
3 BAKE at 400°F for 20 minutes, until meatballs are cooked through.

15-MINUTE STROGANOFFS

>> **KRAFT KITCHENS TIP**
Reduced-fat sour cream and
light cream cheese spread
make great substitutes in
this dish.

Just follow our 3 simple steps:

1 COOK **meat** (1 lb should do it for 4) and 1 onion, chopped, in a large skillet with a little oil. Add **veggies/fruit** (a handful per person).

2 ADD 2 cups **broth** and 2 cups uncooked wide egg noodles. Bring to boil; cover. Reduce heat and simmer 10 minutes. Remove from heat.

3 STIR in 1 cup sour cream or 1 tub (8 oz) cream cheese spread; cover. Let stand 5 minutes.

And use the ingredients you have on hand …

What **meat** do you feel like?	What **veggies/fruit** do you have on hand?	Add the **broth**
boneless, skinless chicken, sliced	pepper strips	chicken
sirloin steak, sliced	sliced mushrooms	beef
pork tenderloin, sliced	sliced apples	chicken
meatless	sliced mushrooms, frozen mixed veggies	vegetable

SPEEDY À LA KING SUPPERS

Just follow our 2 simple steps:

1 PLACE 1 tub (8 oz) cream cheese spread, ½ cup milk, **meat** and a couple handfuls of chopped **veggies** in saucepan; cook on medium for 8-10 minutes or until heated through, stirring occasionally.

2 SERVE over your favorite **base**.

And use the ingredients you have on hand …

What **meat** do you feel like?	Now for the **veggies**	Serve over this **base**
2 cups chopped cooked chicken	chopped peppers, frozen peas (thawed)	frozen puff pastry shells, baked
1 can (6 oz) tuna, drained and flaked	small broccoli florets, chopped onion	cooked noodles
2 cups chopped ham	frozen mixed vegetables (thawed)	toast
meatless	sliced mushrooms and zucchini, chopped pepper	cooked rice

STOVE TOP ONE-DISH CHICKEN BAKE

>> TRY THIS, TOO

Top chicken with 2 cups
frozen mixed vegetables,
thawed, before covering
with soup mixture.

You can also use reduced-
fat sour cream in this dish.

1 package (6 oz) or 2 packages (120 g *each*) Stove Top Stuffing Mix for Chicken
¼ cup butter or margarine, cut up
1-½ cups hot water
4 boneless, skinless chicken breast halves (about 1-¼ lb)
1 can (10-¾ oz) condensed cream of mushroom soup
⅓ cup sour cream or milk

1 MIX contents of stuffing mix pouch, butter and hot water; set aside.
Place chicken in 9– x 13–inch baking dish.
2 MIX soup and sour cream; pour over chicken. Top with stuffing
mixture.
3 BAKE at 375°F for 35 minutes or until chicken is cooked through.
Serves 4.

20-MINUTE STUFFING SKILLET

Just follow our 3 simple steps:

1 MELT a little butter or margarine in large nonstick skillet on medium–high heat. Add **meat** (1 lb should do it for 4); cover. Cook 4 minutes on each side or until cooked through. Remove from skillet.

2 ADD 1-⅔ cups water and a few handfuls **veggies**; bring to boil. Stir in 1 package (6 oz) or 2 packages (120 g *each*) Stove Top Stuffing Mix, any flavor, just to moisten. Return meat to skillet. Season with salt and pepper to taste.

3 SPOON **sauce** over meat; sprinkle with **Kraft Shredded Cheese**; cover. Cook on low heat 5 minutes.

And use the ingredients you have on hand …

What **meat** do you feel like?	What **veggies** do you have on hand?	Try these **sauces** and **Kraft Shredded Cheeses**
boneless, skinless chicken breasts	canned or thawed frozen mixed vegetables	prepared gravy, Cheddar
boneless, skinless chicken breasts	chopped peppers	salsa, Mexican Style cheese
boneless pork chops	corn	barbecue sauce, Cheddar
meatless (use 6-8 oz Portobello mushroom slices*)	chopped zucchini	mushroom gravy, Swiss

*cooked in butter 2 minutes, stirring occasionally

30-MINUTE POT PIES

>> **SHARING OUR EXPERIENCES**
When I entertain, I make the taste of this pleasing dish a little more sophisticated by substituting dry white wine for the milk.
—Susanne, Kraft Kitchens

Just follow our 3 simple steps:

1 MIX 2 cups frozen mixed vegetables, cubed cooked **meat** (leftovers are great here) and **sauce** ingredients in 9-inch pie plate or 2-qt baking dish.

2 PREPARE **topping**; arrange over meat mixture.

3 BAKE at 350°F for 30 minutes.

And use the ingredients you have on hand …

What **meat** do you feel like?	What **sauce** do you like?	Now for the **topping**
chicken	1 can (10-3/4 oz) condensed cream of chicken soup and 1/4 cup milk	1 frozen pie shell, inverted over filling
ham	Cheez Whiz (about 1 cup)	i can (10 oz) refrigerated biscuits, cut into quarters
turkey	1 can (10-3/4 oz) condensed cream of mushroom soup and 1/4 cup milk	1 package (6 oz) stuffing mix, any flavor
meatless (use cubed tofu)	1 can (10-3/4 oz) condensed cream of broccoli soup and 1/4 cup milk	frozen puff pastry, thawed, rolled and cut to fit top of baking dish

30-Minute Chicken Pot Pie

EASY PLEASING MEATLOAF

Just follow our 3 simple steps:

1 MIX 2 lb lean ground beef or ground turkey, 1 cup water, 1 package (6 oz) or 2 packages (120 g *each*) Stove Top Stuffing Mix, any variety, 2 eggs, beaten, and ¼ cup barbecue sauce.

2 SHAPE meat mixture into oval loaf and place in 9-x 13-inch baking dish; top with additional ¼ cup barbecue sauce.

3 BAKE at 375°F for 1 hour or until center is no longer pink.

SIMPLE SHEPHERDS' PIES

>> TRY THIS, TOO
Try homemade biscuit
topping with the steak pie,
mashed sweet potatoes
with the ham version
or cooked rice with the
ground beef pie.

Just follow our 3 simple steps:

1 BROWN **meat** (1 lb should do it for 4) in ovenproof skillet; drain fat.

2 ADD a few handfuls of sliced **veggies** and 1 cup **Kraft Dressing** to meat mixture; cook and stir until veggies are tender. Top generously with homemade mashed potatoes (leftovers work well) or prepared instant mashed potatoes.

3 BROIL 5 minutes or until mashed potatoes are lightly brown on surface.

And use the ingredients you have on hand …

What **meat** do you feel like?	Now for the **veggies**	And try this **Kraft Dressing**
ground beef	sliced carrots, corn	Classic Caesar
chopped ham	green beans, sliced mushrooms	Ranch
sliced sirloin	broccoli florets, sliced carrots	Catalina
meatless	cauliflower florets, chopped peppers and sliced zucchini	Peppercorn Ranch

Shepherds' Pie with Ground Beef

EASY SKILLET CHICKEN

Just follow our 3 simple steps:

1 MOISTEN 6 boneless, skinless chicken breast halves with water; shake off excess.

2 SHAKE chicken, 1 or 2 pieces at a time, in Shake'N Bake Original Chicken Seasoned Coating Mix. Discard any remaining coating mix and bag.

3 HEAT a spoonful of oil in large skillet on medium heat. Add chicken. Cook 7 minutes; turn. Cook an additional 7-8 minutes or until chicken is cooked through.

Easy Skillet Chicken is also terrific in the following ways:

EASY SKILLET CHICKEN WITH LEMON SAUCE

Prepare as directed. Mix equal parts sour cream and mayonnaise. Stir in a few spoonfuls lemon juice. Serve over chicken.

EASY SKILLET MEXICAN CHICKEN

Prepare as directed. Top chicken with 1 cup salsa and 1 cup Mexican-style shredded cheese; cover. Cook an additional 2-4 minutes or until cheese is melted.

>> KRAFT KITCHENS TIP
Chicken pieces can be coated and stored in the refrigerator until ready to cook, up to 1 day in advance.

You can also use reduced-fat sour cream and light mayonnaise in the Lemon Sauce version of this dish.

Easy Skillet Chicken with Lemon Sauce

BAKED CATALINA CHICKEN

>> **KRAFT KITCHENS TIPS**
Catalina Chicken will likely make enough for 2 meals – share half your cooking with a friend who has recently had a baby or is just home after a hospital stay.

Catalina Chicken reheats well in a microwave oven or in a conventional oven.

Just follow our 3 simple steps:

1 PLACE 5-6 lb chicken pieces in 2 (9- x 13-inch) baking pans.

2 MIX 1 can (16 oz) whole-berry cranberry sauce, 1 bottle (8 oz) Kraft Catalina Dressing and 1 package (2 oz) dry onion-soup mix; pour evenly over chicken.

3 BAKE at 350°F for 1 hour or until cooked through.

OVEN-BAKED FISH AND CHIPS

Just follow our 3 simple steps:

1 SHAKE 1 block frozen fish in original or extra-crispy seasoned coating mix.

2 PLACE on baking sheet with 1 package (24 oz) frozen potato wedges.

3 BAKE at 450°F for 20 minutes or until fish flakes easily and potatoes are golden brown.

3-STEP CHILI DINNERS

Just follow our 3 simple steps:

1 COOK ground **meat** (1 lb should do it for 4) and a few handfuls of sliced **veggies** in ¼ cup Italian dressing until meat is cooked and veggies are tender.

2 ADD 1 can (19 oz) *each* undrained diced tomatoes and kidney beans and a few dashes *each* garlic powder and chili powder. Bring to boil. Reduce heat to medium-low; simmer 10 minutes.

3 STIR in a few handfuls of **Kraft Shredded Cheese**; cook until melted. Top with additional cheese just before serving.

And use the ingredients you have on hand …

>> TRY THIS, TOO
3-Step Chili tastes great with our 5-Ingredient Cheddar Biscuits (page 53).

What ground **meat** do you feel like?	What **veggies** do you have on hand?	Add this **Kraft Shredded Cheese**
chicken	sliced mushrooms and carrots	Italian Style
beef	chopped onions and peppers	Mexican Style
pork	sliced celery and zucchini	Cheddar
meatless (use 1 cup rice)	corn, sliced celery and chopped onion	Mexican Style

SLOW-COOKER BEEF STEWS

Just follow our 3 simple steps:

1 ADD cubes of stewing beef (2 lb should do it for 4) and a chopped onion to slow-cooker container.

2 ADD **veggies** (a couple handfuls of *each*) and **sauce** ingredients (1 cup of *each*) to meat mixture; cover with lid.

3 COOK on LOW setting for 6-7 hours or until meat is cooked through and veggies are tender. Finish with one of our **serving suggestions**.

And use the ingredients you have on hand …

Try these **veggies**	Add these **sauce** ingredients	And choose a **serving suggestion**
sliced mushrooms, cut green beans	regular barbecue sauce, beef broth	stir in spoonful of sour cream, serve over noodles
sliced celery and mushrooms	barbecue sauce with onion bits, dry red wine	serve over rice
sliced squash, chopped peppers	spicy barbecue sauce, beef broth	stir in corn, top with cheese and tortilla chips
sliced carrots and celery	sweet-and-sour sauce, chicken broth	serve with rice, top with chow mein noodles

Beef Stew with Carrots and Celery

SLOW-SIMMERED SLOPPY JOES

Just follow our 3 simple steps:

1 BROWN lean ground beef or ground turkey (2 lb should do for 8) in large skillet; drain.

2 MIX meat, **sauce** and ½ cup water in slow-cooker; cover with lid.

3 COOK on LOW setting for 4-6 hours. Fill split hamburger buns with meat mixture and **Kraft Cheese**.

And use the ingredients you have on hand …

Try one of these **sauces**	Try this **Kraft Cheese**
1 bottle (18 oz) barbecue sauce	Cheez Whiz
1 jar (16 oz) salsa and 1 package (1-1/4 oz) taco-seasoning mix	Mexican Style Shredded
1 jar (14 oz) spaghetti sauce	Shredded Mozzarella
1 bottle (14 oz) ketchup and 1 tablespoon mustard	Kraft Singles

>> TRY THIS, TOO
This recipe is delicious made with ground turkey instead of ground beef.

>> KRAFT KITCHENS TIP
Don't peek. Removing the slow-cooker lid releases heat and lengthens the cooking time.

Sloppy Joe with Mozzarella

ALL-AMERICAN DELUXE CHEESEBURGERS

Just follow our 3 simple steps:

1 MIX 1 lb ground beef with **seasoning/sauce** and shape into 4 patties.

2 COOK patties in skillet on medium heat, 4-6 minutes on each side or until cooked through. Top each patty with Kraft Singles; cover. Continue to heat until Singles are melted.

3 GARNISH with lettuce, tomato and your favorite **toppings**. Serve on toasted Kaiser or hamburger rolls.

And use the ingredients you have on hand …

Which **seasoning/sauce** do you feel like?	And now for the **toppings**
1 package (1-1/4 oz) taco-seasoning mix	salsa
2 tablespoons barbecue sauce	barbecue sauce and crisply cooked bacon
2 tablespoons pizza sauce	pizza sauce and sliced pepperoni
2 tablespoons ketchup	ketchup, mustard and pickles

All-American Deluxe Bacon Cheeseburger

EASY DINNER MELTS

Just follow our 3 simple steps:

1 MIX chopped **meat** with a couple spoonfuls of Miracle Whip, a few handfuls of **Kraft Shredded Cheese** and **add-ins**. Spread on favorite bread (such as English muffins, crusty rolls, bagels, pizza crust).

2 BAKE at 400°F for 20 minutes.

3 ADD extra toppings (see our kitchen tip) and serve.

And use the ingredients you have on hand …

>> KRAFT KITCHENS TIP
Dill pickles, sliced avocado, lettuce and tomato all make great toppings to these Easy Dinner Melts.

What **meat** do you feel like?	Add some **Kraft Shredded Cheese**	And now for the **add-ins**
cooked chicken	Mexican Style	sliced green onion and salsa
cooked turkey	Mozzarella	chopped green onion
cooked ham	Italian Style	chopped pickle
meatless (use hard-cooked egg)	Cheddar	pinch of dry mustard

Ham-and-Pickle Dinner Melt

15-MINUTE SOFT TACOS

Just follow our 3 simple steps:

1 BROWN lean ground **meat** (1 lb should do it for 4) in large nonstick skillet.

2 STIR IN 2 cups *each* water and Minute White Rice and 1 package (1-¼ oz) taco-seasoning mix. Bring to boil.

3 SPRINKLE with Mexican-style shredded cheese, let stand 5 minutes. Spoon meat mixture evenly onto flour tortillas, then add sliced **veggies** and **topping**.

And use the ingredients you have on hand …

What ground **meat** do you feel like?	What **veggies** do you have on hand?	And now for the **topping**
chicken	tomatoes, peppers	salsa
beef	peppers, corn	guacamole
pork	tomatoes, onions	salsa
meatless (use 1 can/19 oz kidney beans, drained)	tomatoes, green onions	sour cream

CHEESY QUESADILLAS

Just follow our 2 simple steps:

1 PLACE 1 tortilla on microwavable plate. Place **Kraft Cheese** on half of tortilla, then add a small handful *each* of chopped **meat** and **veggies**. Fold tortilla in half to cover cheese. Cover.

2 MICROWAVE on HIGH 25-40 seconds or until cheese begins to melt. Let stand, covered, 1 minute or until cool enough to eat. Serve with salsa.

And use the ingredients you have on hand …

>> **SHARING OUR EXPERIENCES**
My boys enjoy it when I serve Cheesy Quesadillas with crisp apple slices, celery sticks and some dressing alongside as a dip.
—Tracy, Kraft Kitchens

What **Kraft Cheese** do you feel like?	Add the **meat**	And now for the **veggies**
Cheez Whiz	cooked bacon	onions, peppers
Kraft Singles	cooked chicken	tomatoes, avocados
Shredded Cheddar	pepperoni	black olives, peppers
Mexican Style Shredded	meatless	black beans, corn, green onions

Cheesy Quesadillas with Tomato and Avocado

SIMPLE SANDWICH FILLINGS

Just follow our 2 simple steps:

1 MIX ½ cup Miracle Whip with chopped cooked **meat** (½ lb should do it for 4 sandwiches), 2 stalks celery, chopped, and 2 green onions, chopped.

2 ADD a handful of chopped **add-ins** and a spoonful of **flavoring**. Use as sandwich filling or serve with crackers.

And use the ingredients you have on hand …

What **meat** do you feel like?	What **add-ins** do you have on hand?	And now for the **flavoring**
chicken	toasted almonds	sweetened dried cranberries
tuna	green apple, raisins	curry powder
salmon	teriyaki sauce	ground ginger
meatless (use 4 hard-cooked eggs)	tomatoes	ground cumin

Nearly everyone has a favorite sweet, and some of us have a few more than just one or two. In this handy easy-to-follow cookbook, we've collected a wide range of old favorites to satisfy almost every personal preference. Luscious cheesecakes, chocolate goodies in many guises, a whole range of Jell-O treats, puddings, cakes, squares and more can be found in the pages just ahead.

Desserts

Desserts don't have to be difficult - now you can enjoy time with your guests, too. Savor every bite: A little bit can go a long way to satisfy your sweet tooth. If a batch of child-pleasing cookies or a layer cake guaranteed to make you feel nostalgic is on the agenda, all you have to do is read on. If butter tarts, an apple pie or moist muffins are what you're after, you need look no further. Just read on, and satisfy that craving for something sweet right now. Before you know it, those goodies will be ready to enjoy. And don't forget the coffee!

Previous page: From an ad for Maxwell House Coffee, 1981.

CLASSIC COOKIE CRUSTS

Just follow our 2 simple steps:

1 MIX **cookies,** finely crushed (about 1-¼ cups crumbs), ¼ cup sugar and ⅓ cup melted butter or margarine in small bowl; press mixture firmly onto bottom and up inside of 9-inch pie plate.

2 BAKE at 375°F for 8-10 minutes. Cool completely. Use as a base with any of the suggested **fillings.**

And use the ingredients you have on hand …

>> **KRAFT KITCHENS TIP**
To crush cookies, place in large sealable plastic bag, squeeze out air and seal. Run rolling pin back and forth over surface. Or crush in food processor or blender.

What **cookie** do you feel like?	How many cookies do you need?	Great **filling** ideas
chocolate sandwich	15	chocolate-chip ice cream
vanilla wafer	35	butter-pecan ice cream
graham cracker	14-16 squares	vanilla pudding
gingersnap	20	butterscotch pudding

CHEDDAR-CRUST APPLE PIE

>> **KRAFT KITCHENS TIP**
Rolling the crust between
2 sheets of waxed paper
prevents sticking and makes
it easier to transfer the
crust to the pie plate.

1-1/2 cups flour
1/2 cup shortening
1-1/2 cups shredded Cheddar cheese
4 to 6 tablespoons water
1/2 cup sugar
2 tablespoons flour
1/2 teaspoon ground cinnamon
6 cups sliced peeled apples
2 tablespoons butter or margarine

1 MIX 1-1/2 cups flour and shortening with pastry blender or 2 forks until mixture resembles coarse crumbs. Stir in cheese.

2 ADD water; mix lightly with fork. Form into ball. Divide dough in half. Roll one half to 11-inch circle on lightly floured surface. Place in 9-inch pie plate.

3 MIX sugar, 2 tablespoons flour and cinnamon. Toss with apples; place in pie shell. Dot with butter. Roll out remaining pastry to 11-inch circle; place over apple filling. Seal and flute edge. Cut several slits to permit steam to escape. Bake at 425°F for 35 minutes or until golden brown. *Serves 8.*

RITZ MOCK APPLE PIE

Pastry for double-crust pie
36 Ritz Crackers, coarsely broken (about 1-¾ cups crumbs)
2 cups sugar
1-¾ cups water
2 teaspoons cream of tartar
2 tablespoons lemon juice
Grated peel of 1 lemon
2 tablespoons butter or margarine
Few dashes ground cinnamon

1 PLACE 1 pie crust in 9-inch pie plate. Place cracker crumbs in crust.
2 HEAT sugar, water and cream of tartar to boil in saucepan on high heat.
Reduce heat to medium-low; simmer 15 minutes. Add lemon juice and
peel; cool. Pour syrup over cracker crumbs. Dot with butter; sprinkle with
cinnamon. Place remaining crust over pie. Slit top and trim edges. Pinch
edges with fork to seal.
3 BAKE at 425°F for 30-35 minutes or until crust is golden. Cool completely.
Serves 10.

>> **INSIDE A CLASSIC**
Mock Apple Pie's popularity
soared during World War II,
when fresh apples were hard
to come by.

ANY FRUIT PIES

>> TRY THIS, TOO
Any Fruit Pies can also be made with a ready-made cookie crust.

Just follow our 3 simple steps:

1 MIX 1-½ cups finely crushed **cookie crumbs** and ⅓ cup melted butter or margarine. Press onto bottom and up inside of 9-inch pie plate.

2 DISSOLVE 1 package (4-serving size) **gelatin** in ¾ cup boiling water. Add 2 cups ice cubes. Stir until gelatin is thickened; remove any unmelted ice.

3 ADD 2 cups thawed whipped topping and a cupful of fresh or canned **fruit**, drained; stir gently. Refrigerate 10 minutes or until filling is thick. Spoon into prepared crust. Refrigerate until filling is set.

And use the ingredients you have on hand …

What **cookie crumbs** do you feel like?	Try this flavor of **gelatin**	And now for the **fruit**
chocolate sandwich	cherry	pitted sweet cherries
graham cracker	strawberry	strawberries, raspberries and/or blueberries
graham cracker	lemon	sliced peeled apricots
vanilla wafer	orange	sliced peeled peaches

Any Fruit Peach Pie and Mixed Berry Pie

CREAMY DOUBLE-LAYER PIE

Just follow our 3 simple steps:

1 POUR 1-¾ cups cold milk into large bowl. Add 2 packages (4-serving size *each*) **Jell-O Instant Pudding & Pie Filling**. Beat 2 minutes with wire whisk or until well blended. Gently stir in 2 cups thawed whipped topping.

2 SPOON into 9-inch prepared **crumb crust** (page 107) .

3 SPREAD additional whipped topping over pudding. Refrigerate 3 hours or until set. Add finishing **topping**.

And use the ingredients you have on hand …

>> **KRAFT KITCHENS TIP**
Make this delicious dessert in even less time by using a ready-made crumb crust.

What flavor **Jell-O Instant Pudding & Pie Filling?**	Pour into this **crumb crust**	Finish with this **topping**
chocolate	chocolate	chopped chocolate wafers
vanilla	gingersnap	sliced strawberries
lemon	vanilla wafer	fresh blueberries
butterscotch	graham cracker	caramel sauce

CLASSIC BUTTER TARTS

>> **CHOCOLATE BUTTER TARTS**

Omit raisins. Chop 3 squares of bittersweet chocolate into 12 pieces. Place 1 chunk on bottom of each tart shell before filling and baking. Drizzle baked tarts with more melted chocolate.

Just follow our 3 simple steps:

1 MIX ¾ cup packed brown sugar, ¼ cup corn syrup, 1 egg, 2 tablespoons softened butter or margarine, 1 teaspoon vanilla and a handful of raisins.

2 SPOON into 12 unbaked medium tart shells, filling ¾ full.

3 BAKE at 450°F for 12-14 minutes or until filling is puffed and bubbly and pastry is light golden. Let cool on racks.

>> **KRAFT KITCHENS TIP** Make your own tart shells: Cut 12 (4-inch) circles from 1 package (15 oz) refrigerated pie crust (2 crusts; 6 circles per crust). Line 12 muffin tins with pie-crust circles, pressing the crust onto the bottom and inside of each cup and forming lip at the top of each. Fill and bake as directed. Run a sharp knife around edges of each tin to loosen tarts, if necessary.

HEAVENLY CHOCOLATE CAKE

CAKE
1 package (2-layer size) chocolate cake mix (not pudding-in-the-mix variety)
½ cup unsweetened cocoa
3 eggs
1-⅓ cups water
1 cup Miracle Whip
FROSTING
1 package (8 oz) cream cheese, softened
2 tablespoons milk
1 teaspoon vanilla
5 cups sifted powdered sugar
½ cup unsweetened cocoa

For the cake:
1 STIR cake mix and ½ cup cocoa in a bowl. Add eggs, water and Miracle Whip; beat on low speed 30 seconds, scraping bowl often. Beat on medium speed 2 minutes. Grease and flour 2 (9-inch) round cake pans. Line bottoms of pans with waxed paper. Pour batter into pans.
2 BAKE at 350°F for 30–35 minutes or until toothpick inserted in center comes out clean. Cool 10 minutes; remove from pans and immediately peel off waxed paper. Cool completely on wire racks.
For the frosting:
3 BEAT cream cheese, milk and vanilla until well blended. Mix sugar and remaining ½ cup cocoa. Gradually add to cream cheese mixture, beating well after each addition. Fill and frost cake layers. *Serves 16.*

>> **KRAFT KITCHEN TIP**
Make it a single-layer cake: Use greased and floured 9- x 13-inch baking pan. Bake at 350°F for 35-40 minutes or until toothpick inserted in center comes out clean. Cool completely. Spread frosting over cake.

RUM-NUT PUDDING CAKE

>> **KRAFT KITCHENS TIP**
To make warm syrup for
Rum-Nut Pudding Cake,
mix 1 cup sugar, ½ cup
butter or margarine and
¼ cup water in saucepan.
Cook, stirring frequently,
until mixture comes
to a boil; boil 5 minutes.
Slowly add ½ cup rum.
Pour over cake.

Just follow our 3 simple steps:

1 SPRINKLE a handful of chopped pecans onto bottom of greased fluted tube pan.

2 BEAT 1 package (4-serving size) vanilla instant pudding-and-pie filling, 1 package (2-layer size) white cake mix, 4 eggs and ½ cup *each* water, oil and rum in large bowl with electric mixer.

3 POUR into pan and bake at 350°F for about 50 minutes. Cool slightly. Remove cake from pan, prick with wooden pick or fork. Pour warm syrup over cake.

EASY FROSTED CARROT CAKE

Just follow our 3 simple steps:

1 PREPARE 1 package (2-layer size) carrot cake mix as directed on package for 9- x 13-inch baking pan. Cool completely.

2 BEAT 1 package (8 oz) cream cheese, softened, ⅓ cup sugar and ¼ cup milk until well blended. Gently stir in 4 cups thawed whipped topping. Spread over top of cake.

3 REFRIGERATE until ready to serve. Garnish as desired.

>> **TRY THIS, TOO** You can substitute spice cake mix for carrot cake mix and stir in 4 grated carrots to make an equally pleasing spicy variation.

JELL-O POKE CAKE

Just follow our 3 simple steps:
1 PLACE 2 baked 9-inch round white cake layers, cooled, top sides up, in 2 clean 9-inch round cake pans. Pierce cake with fork at ½-inch intervals.
2 STIR 1 cup boiling water into 1 package (4-serving size) any flavor Jell-O Gelatin. Repeat with 1 cup boiling water and different flavor Jell-O Gelatin in separate bowl. Carefully pour 1 flavor of gelatin over each cake layer.
3 REFRIGERATE 3 hours. Dip 1 cake pan in warm water 10 seconds. Unmold onto serving plate. Frost top with about 1 cup whipped topping. Unmold second cake layer; carefully place on first layer. Frost top and sides of cake with additional whipped topping.

JELL-O PUDDING POKE CAKE

Just follow our 3 simple steps:
1 PREPARE and bake 1 package (2-layer size) any flavor cake mix as directed on package for 9- x 13-inch baking pan. Remove from oven. Immediately poke large holes down through cake to pan with round handle of a wooden spoon, at 1-inch intervals.
2 POUR 4 cups cold milk into large bowl. Add 2 packages (4-serving size *each*) any flavor Jell-O Instant Pudding & Pie Filling. Beat 2 minutes. Immediately pour half the pudding evenly over warm cake and into holes. Let remaining pudding mixture stand to thicken slightly.
3 FROST cake with remaining pudding.

>> KRAFT KITCHENS TIPS
Refrigerate cake at least 1 hour or until ready to serve. Store leftovers in refrigerator.

Dress up this dessert by sprinkling multi-colored sprinkles, chocolate shavings, chopped nuts or toasted coconut over finished cake.

MIDNIGHT BLISS CAKE

>> KRAFT KITCHENS TIP
To remove cake from pan,
loosen cake from side of pan
with small knife or spatula.
Invert cake onto rack and
gently remove cake.

1 package (2-layer size) chocolate cake mix
1 package (4-serving size) chocolate instant pudding-and-pie filling
½ cup French vanilla instant-coffee drink mix
4 eggs
1 cup sour cream
½ cup *each* oil and water
1 package (8 oz) Baker's Semi-Sweet Baking Chocolate, chopped

1 PLACE cake mix, pudding mix, coffee mix, eggs, sour cream, oil and water in large bowl. Beat with electric mixer on low speed just until moistened. Beat on medium speed 2 minutes or until well blended. Stir in chocolate.
2 POUR into lightly greased and floured 12-cup fluted tube pan or 10-inch tube pan.
3 BAKE at 350°F for 50–60 minutes or until toothpick inserted near center comes out clean. Cool 10 minutes on wire rack. Remove from pan. Sprinkle with powdered sugar, if desired. *Serves 12.*

Midnight Bliss Cake; in back, Rum-Nut Pudding Cake and Heavenly Chocolate Cake

RED VELVET CAKE

CAKE
1 package (2-layer size) white cake mix
2 squares unsweetened baking chocolate, melted
2 tablespoons red food coloring
FROSTING
1 package (8 oz) cream cheese, softened
½ cup butter or margarine, softened
1 package (16 oz) powdered sugar

>> **INSIDE A CLASSIC**
The Red Velvet Cake is
especially popular in the
southern United States,
even though it originated
at the Waldorf-Astoria
Hotel in New York City.

For the cake:
1 PREPARE and bake cake mix as directed on package for 9- x 13-inch pan, adding chocolate and food coloring (along with amounts of water, eggs and oil specified on the package); cool completely.
For the frosting:
2 BEAT cream cheese and butter until well blended, to prepare frosting. Gradually add sugar, beating until smooth. Spread on cake. *Serves 12.*

>> **TRY THIS, TOO** Sprinkle with ½ cup chopped pecans as a special treat.

PHILADELPHIA 3-STEP CHEESECAKE

>> **KRAFT KITCHENS TIP**
To make a party-sized
cheesecake: Mix 2 cups
crushed graham crackers,
⅓ cup sugar and 6 table-
spoons melted butter or
margarine. Press on bottom
of 9- x 13-inch glass baking
dish. Double the recipe
for cheesecake filling, pour
over crust and bake at
325°F for 40–50 minutes
or until center is almost set.
Cool and serve as directed.

Just follow our 3 simple steps:

1 BEAT 2 packages (8 oz *each*) Philadelphia Cream Cheese, softened; ½ cup sugar, ½ teaspoon vanilla and **add-ins** until smooth. Add 2 eggs, 1 at a time; mix until just blended.

2 POUR into ready-to-use graham cracker crust. Sprinkle with **toppers**.

3 BAKE at 325°F for 40-45 minutes or until center is almost set. Cool. Refrigerate 3 hours or overnight. Serve with a dollop of whipped topping.

And use the ingredients you have on hand …

Choose these **add-ins**	And now for the **toppers**
1/2 teaspoon grated lemon peel	sliced assorted fresh fruit, drizzled with warm apple jelly or strawberry jam*
4 squares semisweet chocolate, melted	miniature marshmallows, semisweet chocolate chunks and chopped peanuts
1/2 cup canned pumpkin, dash *each* ground cinnamon ground cloves and nutmeg	chocolate-covered English toffee bars, coarsely chopped
a few handfuls mini chocolate-sandwich cookies	semisweet chocolate, melted, with a little whipping cream*

*top after baking

Fruit-Topped Lemon 3-Step Cheesecake

CLASSIC NEW YORK CHEESECAKE

CRUST
1 cup graham cracker crumbs
3 tablespoons sugar
3 tablespoons butter or margarine, melted
FILLING
5 packages (8 oz *each*) Philadelphia Cream Cheese, softened
1 cup sugar
3 tablespoons flour
1 tablespoon vanilla
1 cup sour cream
3 eggs
1 can (21 oz) cherry pie filling

>> INSIDE A CLASSIC
Philadelphia Brand cream cheese was introduced in 1880, named as a tribute to Philadelphia, which was considered a home to fine food.

For the crust:
1 MIX graham cracker crumbs, 3 tablespoons sugar and butter. Press firmly onto bottom of 9-inch springform pan. Bake at 350°F for 10 minutes.
For the filling:
2 BEAT cream cheese, 1 cup sugar, flour and vanilla until well blended. Blend in sour cream. Add eggs, 1 at a time, mixing on low speed after each addition just until blended. Pour over crust.
3 BAKE at 350°F for 1 hour or until center is almost set. Run knife around rim of pan to loosen cake; cool before removing rim of pan. Refrigerate 4 hours or overnight. Top with pie filling just before serving. *Serves 16.*

STRIPED DELIGHT

½ cup butter or margarine, melted
1 cup flour
2 tablespoons sugar
Chopped nuts
1 package (8 oz) cream cheese, softened
1 cup powdered sugar
2 cups thawed Cool Whip Whipped Topping
1 package (4-serving size) chocolate instant pudding-and-pie filling
1 package (4-serving size) vanilla instant pudding-and-pie filling
3 cups milk, divided

1 MIX butter, flour, sugar and a handful of nuts. Press into 9- x 13-inch baking dish. Bake at 325°F for 15 minutes. Cool.
2 BEAT cream cheese and sugar until well blended. Spread over crust. Cover with whipped topping.
3 PREPARE each pudding mix with 1-½ cups milk in a separate bowl. Pour chocolate pudding over whipped-topping layer; top with layer of vanilla pudding. Top with additional whipped topping and refrigerate until ready to serve. Top with shaved semisweet baking chocolate. *Serves 16.*

FRUITY PHILADELPHIA FREEZE

Just follow our 3 simple steps:

1 MIX 1 cup finely crushed **cookie crumbs** with ¼ cup butter or margarine, melted. Press onto bottom of 9-inch square pan lined with foil.
2 BEAT 2 tubs (8 oz *each*) **Philadelphia Cream Cheese Spread** until creamy. Gradually add 1 can (12 oz) frozen **juice concentrate**, thawed, beating well. Add 1 tub (8 oz) thawed whipped topping; beat until well blended.
3 POUR over crust. Freeze several hours or until firm. Remove from freezer 15 minutes before serving.

And use the ingredients you have on hand …

What **cookie crumbs** do you feel like?	Try this **Philadelphia Cream Cheese Spread**	Add this **juice concentrate**
chocolate sandwich	strawberry	raspberry
graham cracker	pineapple	lemonade
vanilla wafer	plain	lime
chocolate sandwich	plain	fruit punch

CHOCOLATE PLUNGE

>> DESSERT DIP
Mix 1 package (8 oz)
Philadelphia Cream Cheese,
softened, and 1 jar (7 oz)
marshmallow creme
until well blended; cover.
Refrigerate several hours
or until chilled.

Just follow our 2 simple steps:

1 MIX ⅔ cup light corn syrup and ½ cup whipping cream in large microwavable bowl. Microwave on HIGH 1-½ minutes or until mixture comes to boil. Add 1 package (8 oz) Baker's Semi-Sweet Baking Chocolate; stir until chocolate is completely melted.

2 SERVE warm, as a dip, with assorted fresh fruit such as strawberries, apple, cherries, nectarines, pineapple or banana; cookies, cake cubes or pretzels.

Chocolate Plunge is also terrific in the following ways:

CHOCOLATE PEANUT BUTTER PLUNGE
Prepare as directed. Immediately stir in ½ cup peanut butter until blended.

CHOCOLATE RASPBERRY PLUNGE
Prepare as directed. Immediately stir in ¼ cup seedless raspberry jam.

MOCHA PLUNGE
Prepare as directed. Immediately stir in 1 tablespoon instant coffee granules.

4 WAYS WITH SHORTCAKE

Just follow our 2 simple steps:

1 TOSS 2 cups **fruit** with a few spoonfuls of powdered sugar.

2 PLACE **base** on individual serving plates. Finish with **topping** and fruit.

And use the ingredients you have on hand …

What **fruit** do you feel like?	Choose a **base**	Spoon on this **topping**
sliced peeled peaches	angel food cake, cut in slices	Cool Whip Whipped Topping, thawed
raspberries	pound cake, cut in slices	scoops of ice cream
sliced strawberries	biscuits	Cool Whip Whipped Topping, thawed
blueberries	sponge cake, cut in slices	fruit yogurt

BANANA BREAD

>> **SHARING OUR EXPERIENCES**

Whenever I have an overripe banana, I put it in the freezer. I take it from the freezer to microwave on HIGH 1 minute. The skin slips off and it's ready to use in baking.
—Tracy, Kraft Kitchens

2 eggs

3 bananas, mashed

⅓ cup *each* oil and milk

2 cups flour

½ cup *each* Post 100% Bran Cereal and sugar

2 teaspoons baking powder

1 STIR eggs, bananas, oil and milk until well blended.

2 ADD flour, cereal, sugar and baking powder; stir just until moistened. Pour into lightly greased 9- x 5-inch loaf pan.

3 BAKE at 350°F for 1 hour or until done. Cool 10 minutes; remove from pan. Cool completely on rack. *Serves 16.*

RAISIN BRAN MUFFINS

1-¼ cups flour
1 tablespoon baking powder
2 cups Post Raisin Bran
1 cup milk
1 egg, slightly beaten
½ cup applesauce
⅓ cup packed brown sugar
2 tablespoons margarine, melted

>> **KRAFT KITCHENS TIP**
Here we've created a deliciously moist alternative to a traditional muffin by replacing some of the margarine with applesauce.

1 MIX flour and baking powder in large bowl. Mix cereal and milk in another bowl; let stand 3 minutes. Stir in egg, applesauce, sugar and margarine. Add to flour mixture; stir just until moistened. (Batter will be lumpy.)

2 SPOON batter into muffin pan lined with paper liners, filling each cup two-thirds full.

3 BAKE at 400°F for 20 minutes or until golden brown. Serve warm. *Serves 12.*

CLASSIC RICE PUDDING

Just follow our 3 simple steps:

1 MIX 3-½ cups milk, 1 package (6-serving size) cook-and-serve **pudding-and-pie filling** and 1 cup Minute White Rice in medium saucepan.

2 COOK on medium heat, stirring constantly, until mixture comes to boil. Remove from heat.

3 STIR in a handful of **add-ins**. Cover surface of pudding with plastic wrap; cool 10 minutes. Stir. Serve warm.

And use the ingredients you have on hand …

What flavor of **pudding-and-pie filling?**	Try these **add-ins**
vanilla or coconut cream	raisins or sweetened dried cranberries
chocolate	semisweet chocolate chunks or chips
butterscotch or banana cream	toasted chopped pecans and/or sliced bananas
vanilla	chopped apple and/or dash of cinnamon

Rice Pudding with Sweetened Dried Cranberries

FRUIT CRUMBLE

Just follow our 3 simple steps:

1 MIX ½ cup (half 8-oz tub) **cream cheese spread** and 2 cups crushed **cookies** with fork until mixture resembles coarse crumbs. Do not overmix.

2 SPOON **fruit** into pie plate or individual baking dishes; sprinkle with cookie mixture.

3 BAKE at 400°F for 12-15 minutes or until lightly browned. Serve warm.

And use the ingredients you have on hand …

Try this flavor **cream cheese spread**	Use these crushed **cookies**	Spoon in this **fruit**
strawberry	vanilla wafers	chopped peeled fresh peaches or chopped canned peach slices
honey nut or apple cinnamon	oatmeal raisin	canned apple pie filling
plain	oatmeal	chopped peeled fresh pears or chopped canned pear slices
pineapple	gingersnaps	chopped dried tropical fruit mix

QUICK NILLA BANANA PUDDING

Just follow our 3 simple steps:
1 PREPARE 2 packages (4-serving size *each*) vanilla instant pudding-and-pie filling as directed on package for pudding, using only 3 cups milk.
2 SPOON ½ cup of the pudding onto bottom of large serving bowl. Top with Nilla Wafers, a generous layer of sliced bananas and ⅔ cup pudding. Stand wafers around outside edge of dish. Repeat layers twice; top with layer of pudding. Cover.
3 REFRIGERATE at least 3 hours to soften wafers. Just before serving, spread 2 cups thawed whipped topping over pudding. Top with additional banana slices, if desired.

BAKER'S ONE-BOWL BROWNIES

4 squares Baker's Unsweetened Baking Chocolate
¾ cup butter or margarine
2 cups sugar
3 eggs
1 teaspoon vanilla
1 cup flour
1 cup coarsely chopped pecans

1 LINE 9– x 13-inch baking pan with foil extending over edges to form handles. Grease foil.

2 MICROWAVE chocolate and butter in large microwavable bowl on HIGH 2 minutes or until butter is melted. Stir until chocolate is completely melted. Add sugar; stir until well blended. Add eggs and vanilla; mix well. Stir in flour and pecans until well blended. Spread into prepared pan.

3 BAKE at 350°F for 30–35 minutes or until toothpick inserted in center comes out with fudgy crumbs. Do not overbake. Cool in pan. Lift out of pan onto cutting board. Cut into squares. *Makes 24 brownies.*

>> ROCKY ROAD BROWNIES
Prepare batter as directed; spread into pan. Sprinkle with 1 cup Baker's Semi-Sweet Chocolate Chunks or Chips. Bake as directed. Immediately sprinkle with a few handfuls miniature marshmallows, chopped pecans and Baker's Semi-Sweet Chocolate Chunks or Chips.

NANAIMO BARS

>> **MINTY NANAIMO BARS**
MINTY NANAIMO BARS
Prepare as directed, adding
a few drops green food
coloring and 1 teaspoon
peppermint extract to
pudding mixture.

2 cups crushed chocolate sandwich cookies
1 cup coconut or chopped nuts
½ cup butter or margarine, melted
1 package (4-serving size) vanilla instant pudding-and-pie filling
⅓ cup *each* butter or margarine, softened, and hot water
2 cups powdered sugar
4 squares semisweet baking chocolate, chopped
1 tablespoon butter or margarine

1 MIX cookie crumbs, coconut and ½ cup melted butter. Press firmly onto bottom of 9-inch square pan. Refrigerate until ready to use.

2 BEAT pudding mix, ⅓ cup softened butter and hot water. Add powdered sugar; beat until well blended. Spread over crust. Refrigerate 2 hours or until filling is set.

3 MICROWAVE chocolate and 1 tablespoon butter on HIGH for 1 minute. Stir until chocolate is completely melted. Spread over pudding layer; refrigerate until set. Cut into bars to serve. Store leftover dessert in refrigerator. *Makes 16 bars.*

CHOCOLATE BLISS COOKIES

1 package (8 oz) Baker's Semi-Sweet Baking Chocolate
¾ cup firmly packed brown sugar
¼ cup butter, softened, or margarine
2 eggs
1 teaspoon vanilla
½ cup flour
¼ teaspoon baking powder
1 package (8 oz) Baker's Semi-Sweet Baking Chocolate, coarsely chopped
   or 1-½ cups Baker's Semi-Sweet Chocolate Chunks
2 cups chopped walnuts

1 MICROWAVE 8 squares chocolate in large microwavable bowl on HIGH 2 minutes. Stir until chocolate is completely melted. Add sugar, butter, eggs and vanilla; stir with wooden spoon until well blended. Add flour and baking powder; mix well. Stir in chopped chocolate and walnuts.
2 DROP scant ¼ cupfuls of dough onto ungreased baking sheets.
3 BAKE at 350°F for 13–14 minutes or until cookies are puffed and feel set to the touch. Cool 1 minute; remove from baking sheets. Cool completely on wire racks. *Makes about 18 large cookies (one cookie per serving).*

>> **KRAFT KITCHENS TIPS**
To make smaller cookies: MIx dough as directed. Drop by heaping tablespoonfuls onto baking sheets. Bake at 350°F for 12-13 minutes. Makes about 30 smaller cookies.

If omitting walnuts, increase flour to ¾ cup to prevent cookies from spreading. Makes about 15 large cookies.

JUMBO OATMEAL COOKIES

1 cup butter or margarine
1-½ cups firmly packed brown sugar
2 eggs
1 teaspoon vanilla
1-½ cups flour
2-½ cups quick-cooking oats
2 teaspoons baking soda
1 package (12 oz) semisweet chocolate chips
1 cup raisins

1 BEAT butter and brown sugar with electric mixer until light and fluffy.
2 ADD eggs and vanilla; mix well. Add flour, oats and baking soda; mix until thoroughly combined. Stir in chocolate chips and raisins. Drop dough in ¼-cup mounds, 3 inches apart, on greased baking sheets. Flatten each cookie into 2-½-inch circle.
3 BAKE at 350°F for 15–16 minutes or until edges are lightly browned. Cool 5 minutes on baking sheets. Transfer to wire racks to cool completely. *Makes 24 cookies.*

SUPER EASY PEANUT BUTTER TREATS

Just follow our 3 simple steps:
1 MIX 1 cup peanut butter, ½ cup sugar and 1 egg until well blended.
2 PICK your favorite variation (see below).
3 BAKE at 325°F for 15–20 minutes or until set. Place on wire racks to cool completely.

Peanut Butter Treats are terrific in the following ways:

SUPER EASY PEANUT BUTTER COOKIES

Prepare peanut butter mixture as directed; stir in a few handfuls chopped white baking chocolate and sweetened dried cranberries. Drop spoonfuls of dough onto baking sheets. Bake as directed.

SUPER EASY PEANUT BUTTER PIE

Prepare peanut butter mixture as directed. Press onto bottom and up inside of 9-inch pie plate. Bake as directed. Meanwhile, prepare 1 package (6-serving size) chocolate cook-and-serve pudding-and-pie filling as directed on package for pie filling. Pour into crust. Refrigerate until set.

SUPER EASY PEANUT BUTTER SQUARES

Prepare peanut butter mixture as directed; press into 8-inch square baking pan. Top with a few handfuls chopped semisweet baking chocolate. Bake as directed. Cool completely before cutting into squares.

>> **KRAFT KITCHENS TIP**
Depending on your personal preference, use creamy, crunchy or reduced-fat peanut butter in this base recipe.

CHOCOLATE-CHUNK COOKIES

>> **CHOCOLATE-CHUNK BARS OR SQUARES**

Spread dough in greased foil-lined 15- x 10- x 1-inch baking pan. Bake at 375°F for 18–20 minutes or until golden brown. (Or bake in 9- x 13-inch baking pan 20–22 minutes.) Cool completely on wire rack.

1-¾ cups flour
¾ teaspoon baking soda
¼ teaspoon salt
¾ cup butter or margarine, softened
½ cup granulated sugar
½ cup firmly packed brown sugar
1 egg
1 teaspoon vanilla
1 package (12 oz) semisweet chocolate chunks or chips
1 cup chopped walnuts or pecans

1 MIX flour, baking soda and salt in medium bowl; set aside.

2 BEAT butter and sugars in large bowl with electric mixer until light and fluffy. Add egg and vanilla; mix well. Gradually beat in flour mixture. Stir in chocolate chunks and walnuts. Drop by heaping tablespoonfuls onto ungreased baking sheets.

3 BAKE at 375°F for 11–13 minutes or just until golden brown. Cool on baking sheets 1 minute. Remove to wire racks; cool completely.
Makes about 36 cookies.

CHOCOLATE-CARAMEL BARS

32 caramels
½ cup evaporated milk
1 cup *each* flour and quick-cooking oats
¾ cup firmly packed brown sugar
½ teaspoon baking soda
¾ cup butter or margarine
½ cup *each* Baker's Semi-Sweet Chocolate Chunks or Chips, and walnuts

1 MELT caramels with evaporated milk in small saucepan on low heat, stirring frequently.

2 MIX flour, oats, brown sugar and baking soda in large bowl. Cut in butter with pastry blender or fork until mixture resembles coarse crumbs.

3 PRESS half the oat mixture into 9-inch square baking pan. Bake at 350°F for 10 minutes. Sprinkle chocolate and walnuts evenly over crust; drizzle with caramel mixture. Sprinkle with remaining oat mixture. Bake an additional 20-25 minutes or until golden brown. Cool completely. Cut into bars. *Makes 16 bars.*

>> **KRAFT KITCHENS TIP**
To melt caramels in the microwave, place caramels and evaporated milk in microwavable bowl. Microwave on HIGH for 2-3 minutes or until caramels are completely melted when stirred.

EASY CEREAL SQUARES

Just follow our 3 simple steps:

1 MELT ¼ cup butter or margarine in large saucepan on low heat. Add 6 cups miniature marshmallows. Cook until marshmallows are completely melted, stirring constantly.

2 ADD 6 cups **Post cereal** and a handful of **add-ins**; mix lightly until cereal is evenly coated with marshmallow mixture.

3 PRESS mixture into 9- x 13-inch pan. Cool; cut into squares.

And use the ingredients you have on hand …

What **Post cereal** do you feel like?	What **add-ins** do you have on hand?
Spoon Size Shredded Wheat	chopped dried apricots
Cocoa Pebbles	semisweet chocolate chunks
Alpha Bits	sweetened dried cranberries
Golden Crisp	raisins

Easy Cereal Squares with Alpha Bits and Sweetened Dried Cranberries

Is there a child anywhere who doesn't have strong feelings about what he thinks tastes good? Personal preferences are all unique, but the Kraft Kitchens have been in the business of pleasing appetites of all ages for quite some time and we know that some of the simplest, most familiar foods enjoy widespread popularity among younger connoisseurs. The recipes featured in the following

Kids' Classics

pages include some of the very best-loved of all these dishes. Consider the appeal of rich and creamy macaroni and cheese with lots of fun variations to suit every youthful appetite, hold-in-your-hand hot-dog roll-ups and some very thick and luscious drinks. You'll also find easy microwave versions of a beloved campfire classic, ice-cream sandwiches the kids can assemble on their own, Gorp squares and even a creamy chocolate fudge with a very surprising secret ingredient. Adults are certain to love them, too – so what are you waiting for?

Previous page: From an ad launching Jell-O Instant Pudding, 1939.

10 WAYS WITH MAC AND CHEESE

Just follow our 2 simple steps:
1 PREPARE 1 package (7-¼ oz) Kraft Macaroni & Cheese Dinner as directed.
2 STIR IN 1 of the add-ins below to make any of 10 terrific variations.

CHEESEBURGER MAC
Cooked ground beef and a small spoonful prepared mustard.

CHICKEN-AND-BROCCOLI MAC
Chopped cooked chicken and cooked broccoli florets.

CHILI MAC
A few spoonfuls leftover chili. Top with shredded Cheddar cheese.

HAM-AND-CHEESE MAC
Chopped ham and finely chopped green onion.

HOT DOG MAC
Corn and chopped cooked wieners.

PIZZA MAC
Chopped pepperoni and chopped tomatoes. Top with shredded mozzarella cheese.

SAUSAGE MAC
Cooked pork sausage, chopped green pepper and onion.

TACO MAC
Cooked seasoned taco meat. Serve with diced tomatoes and shredded lettuce.

TUNA MAC
Drained, flaked canned tuna and thawed frozen peas.

VEGGIE MAC
A few handfuls of your favorite cooked veggies.

CHEESY HOT DOG CRESCENTS

>> MINI HOT DOG CRESCENTS
Substitute 16 cocktail wieners for 8 beef franks. Separate dough into triangles; cut each triangle in half lengthwise. Cut each Singles into 4 strips. Assemble and bake as directed.

Just follow our 2 simple steps:
1 SEPARATE 1 can (8 oz) refrigerated crescent dinner rolls into triangles. Top triangles with 4 Kraft Singles, cut in half diagonally, and 8 beef franks; roll up. Place on baking sheet.
2 BAKE at 375°F for 12 minutes or until golden brown. Serve with your favorite condiments.

EASY HOMEMADE MAC AND CHEESE

Just follow our 2 simple steps:
1 COOK 2 cups elbow macaroni as directed on package; drain. Return to hot pan.
2 ADD 1 lb Velveeta, cut up, and ½ cup milk. Cook on low heat until Velveeta is melted, stirring frequently.

>> SHARING OUR EXPERIENCES I like to add extra zip to my Hot Dog Crescents by spreading 1 teaspoon Dijon or prepared mustard, barbecue sauce or ketchup on each dinner-roll triangle before topping with remaining ingredients. Then I prepare them in the usual way. —Tracy, Kraft Kitchens

GORP SQUARES

¾ cup *each* butter or margarine and firmly packed brown sugar
2 tablespoons light corn syrup
3 cups Post Honey Bunches of Oats Cereal, any flavor
1 cup *each* quick-cooking oats, uncooked, and coconut
¾ cup flour
1 teaspoon baking soda
½ cup *each* raisins, chopped apricots and peanuts

1 COOK butter, sugar and syrup in small saucepan on medium
heat until mixture comes to boil, stirring constantly. Remove from heat.
Immediately add to combined remaining ingredients; mix well.
2 PRESS evenly into lightly greased 15- x 10- x 1-inch baking pan.
3 BAKE at 350°F for 12–15 minutes or until golden brown. Cool slightly.
Cut into squares while warm. *Makes 30 squares.*

VELVEETA FUDGE

¾ lb (12 oz) Velveeta, cut up
1 cup butter or margarine
6 squares unsweetened baking chocolate
2 tablespoons light corn syrup
2 lb powdered sugar, sifted
1-½ cups chopped pecans (optional)
1 teaspoon vanilla

1 PLACE Velveeta, butter, chocolate and corn syrup in 3-qt saucepan; cook and stir on medium-low heat until smooth.
2 GRADUALLY add chocolate mixture to sugar in large bowl, beating until well blended. Stir in pecans and vanilla.
3 SPREAD evenly in greased 9- x 13-inch pan; cover. Refrigerate several hours. Cut into squares. *Makes 3-½ lb.*

>> **KRAFT KITCHENS TIP** Make this fudge ahead of time: Prepare as directed; cool and cut into squares. Wrap tightly. Freeze up to 2 months. Thaw in refrigerator overnight before serving.

JIGGLERS

Just follow our 2 simple steps:

1 STIR 2-½ cups boiling water into 2 packages (8-serving size *each*) or 4 packages (4-serving size *each*) any flavor Jell-O Gelatin in large bowl at least 3 minutes or until completely dissolved. Pour into 9- x 13-inch pan.

2 REFRIGERATE 3 hours or until firm. Dip bottom of pan in warm water for about 15 seconds. Cut into decorative shapes with cookie cutters or cut into 1-inch squares. Lift from pan.

CREAMY JIGGLERS

Just follow our 3 simple steps:

1 STIR 2-½ cups boiling water into 2 packages (8-serving size *each*) any flavor Jell-O Gelatin in large bowl, mixing for at least 3 minutes or until gelatin is completely dissolved. Cool 30 minutes at room temperature.

2 POUR 1 cup cold milk into medium bowl. Add 1 package (4-serving size) Jell-O Vanilla Flavor Instant Pudding & Pie Filling. Beat with wire whisk 1 minute. Quickly pour into gelatin. Stir with wire whisk until well blended. Pour into 9- x 13-inch pan.

3 REFRIGERATE 3 hours or until firm. Dip bottom of pan into warm water for about 15 seconds. Cut into decorative shapes with cookie cutters and lift from pan.

DIRT CUPS

>> SAND CUPS
Prepare as directed, substituting 1 package (12 oz) vanilla wafers and Jell-O Vanilla Instant Pudding & Pie Filling for chocolate cookies and pudding.

Just follow our 3 simple steps:

1 CRUSH 1 package (16 oz) chocolate-sandwich cookies; set aside.

2 POUR 2 cups cold milk into large bowl. Add 1 package (4-serving size) Jell-O Chocolate Instant Pudding & Pie Filling. Beat with wire whisk 2 minutes. Stir in 1 tub (8 oz) whipped topping and half the crushed cookies.

3 PLACE about 1 tablespoon of the remaining crushed cookies in each of 8-10 (7 oz) paper or plastic cups. Fill cups about three-quarters full with pudding mixture. Top with remaining crushed cookies. Refrigerate until ready to serve. Garnish with gummy worms, if desired.

HONEY MAID S'MORES

Just follow our 3 simple steps:

1 BREAK 1 milk chocolate candy bar into 4 pieces; set aside.

2 PLACE 4 Honey Maid Honey Grahams on microwavable plate. Top each with 1 chocolate piece and 1 marshmallow.

3 MICROWAVE on HIGH 15-20 seconds or until marshmallow puffs. Top each with second honey graham; pressing slightly. Serve immediately.

COOKIE SANDWICHES

Just follow our 2 simple steps:

1 SPREAD **cookies** with softened **ice cream**; top each with second cookie.

2 ROLL or lightly press edges into **dippers**. Freeze 4 hours or until firm. Wrap individually in plastic wrap. Store in freezer up to 1 month.

And use the ingredients you have on hand …

What **cookies** do you feel like?	Choose an **ice cream** flavor	And now for the **dippers**
chocolate chip	mint-chocolate chip	miniature chocolate chips
oatmeal	vanilla	raisins
chewy chocolate chip	chocolate chip cookie dough	chocolate sprinkles
peanut butter chocolate chip	chocolate	chopped peanuts

WIND CHILLS

Just follow these 2 simple steps:

1 PLACE 1 qt (4 cups) **frozen yogurt**, softened, ¼–½ cup fat-free milk and 8 **cookies** in blender container; cover. Blend until smooth, occasionally stopping blender to scrape down side of container. Add an extra couple spoonfuls of milk, if the mixture is too thick.

2 POUR into 4 glasses. Serve immediately.

And use the ingredients you have on hand …

What flavor **frozen yogurt** do you feel like?	What **cookies** do you have on hand?
vanilla	Oreo Chocolate Sandwich
chocolate	chocolate chip
vanilla	peanut butter sandwich
strawberry	Raspberry Fig Newtons

Index

NOTES

Recipes everyone liked:

_____
_____
_____
_____
_____
_____
_____
_____
_____
_____
_____
_____
_____
_____
_____
_____
_____
_____
_____
_____
_____

NOTES

Recipes I'd like to try:

_____

_____

_____

_____

_____

_____

_____

_____

_____

_____

_____

_____

_____

_____

_____

_____

_____

_____

_____

_____

_____

NOTES

My favorite tips:

_____

_____

_____

_____

_____

_____

_____

_____

_____

_____

_____

_____

_____

_____

_____

_____

_____

_____

_____

_____

_____